Rebuild! Don't Repair

WHY FIXING THINGS DOESN'T
FIX THINGS IN LIFE

Jon Harper

TRILOGY CHRISTIAN PUBLISHERS
Tustin, CA

Trilogy Christian Publishers
A Wholly Owned Subsidiary of Trinity Broadcasting Network
2442 Michelle Drive
Tustin, CA 92780

Rebuild! Don't Repair

Copyright © 2024 by Jon Harper

Unless otherwise indicated, all scripture quotations are taken from the Holy Bible, New Living Translation, copyright © 1996, 2004, 2015 by Tyndale House Foundation. Used by permission of Tyndale House Publishers, Inc., Carol Stream, Illinois 60188. All rights reserved.

Scripture quotations marked ESV are taken from the ESV® Bible (The Holy Bible, English Standard Version®), copyright © 2001 by Crossway Bibles, a publishing ministry of Good News Publishers. Used by permission. All rights reserved.

Scripture quotations marked NIV are taken from the Holy Bible, New International Version®, NIV®. Copyright © 1973, 1978, 1984, 2011 by Biblica, Inc.™ Used by permission of Zondervan. All rights reserved worldwide. www.zondervan.com. The "NIV" and "New International Version" are trademarks registered in the United States Patent and Trademark Office by Biblica, Inc.™

Scripture quotations marked NKJV are taken from the New King James Version®. Copyright © 1982 by Thomas Nelson. Used by permission.

Scripture quotations marked TLB are taken from The Living Bible copyright © 1971. Used by permission of Tyndale House Publishers, a Division of Tyndale House Ministries, Carol Stream, Illinois 60188. All rights reserved.

Scripture quotations marked KJV are taken from the King James Version of the Bible. Public domain.

All rights reserved, including the right to reproduce this book or portions thereof in any form whatsoever.

For information, address Trilogy Christian Publishing

Rights Department, 2442 Michelle Drive, Tustin, Ca 92780.

Trilogy Christian Publishing/ TBN and colophon are trademarks of Trinity Broadcasting Network.

For information about special discounts for bulk purchases, please contact Trilogy Christian Publishing.

Trilogy Disclaimer: The views and content expressed in this book are those of the author and may not necessarily reflect the views and doctrine of Trilogy Christian Publishing or the Trinity Broadcasting Network.

10 9 8 7 6 5 4 3 2 1

Library of Congress Cataloging-in-Publication Data is available.

ISBN 979-8-89333-665-8

ISBN 979-8-89333-666-5 (ebook)

Dedication

This book is dedicated to my wife, Christina.

Throughout our marriage, your patience with me as I searched for my purpose has been astounding.

Your willingness to allow me time to pour into this book and give the readers what will bring them value is what has made this work possible.

You have always believed in my calling to serve people, and you have been there to support me every step of the way.

I can never thank you enough!

I love you so much!

Acknowledgments

I want to say thank you to Carla Marstall, Lou Anatrella, and my mother and father, who helped me in shaping what this book has become. Your willingness to share your honest thoughts and ideas on this work throughout the process has helped sharpen the message to make an impact on the readers. You all add incredible value to me, which allows me to add value to others. Together, we have created something that will make a difference!

Contents

Introduction vii

Haggai xiv

Answering the Call 1

    Chapter 1. The Limits of Repairing 2

    Chapter 2. Rebuilding versus Repairing 16

Breaking Down 29

    Chapter 3. Your Current Structure 30

    Chapter 4. Demolition Expectations 49

    Chapter 5. Dealing with the Old Foundation 64

    Chapter 6. The Lonely Work: Where Most People Run Back 87

Building Up 104

    Chapter 7. A New Foundation 105

    Chapter 8. The Blessing Begins 116

    Chapter 9. Your New Structure 138

The New You 155

    Chapter 10. The Withholdings 156

    Chapter 11. Passing It On 173

Conclusion 201

About the Author 203

Introduction

When I saw the "T" in the sky, it was obvious this wasn't for me. Bigger things were at work; I just happened to be a piece. Let's go back a bit.

In the summer of 2022, we made a monumental decision to relocate from Florida to Texas. It marked a significant milestone for me, as it was the first time I had ever lived outside of my home state. The catalyst for this move was an unexpected opportunity presented by my boss about four months earlier—a promotion that would require us to uproot our lives and settle in Houston. I was filled with fear at the thought of breaking the news to my wife. After all, we had only recently established ourselves in our first home in St. Augustine, Florida, just a year prior.

Our life there was idyllic—two healthy children, wonderful neighbors, a stable job, and a beautiful home. When I finally mustered the courage to share the news with my wife, it didn't exactly go smoothly. Yet, as we spent the following days in prayerful consideration, we reached a mutual understanding. We decided that I would pursue the promotion, but with a condition—we needed God's guidance.

We prayed fervently, seeking His will for our family. If the promotion was in line with His plan for us, we asked for His blessing; if not, we asked for the door to be closed.

About a month later, we found ourselves making calls to our parents, announcing our impending move. Emotions ran high, but in the uncertainty, we held on to the peace that came from our prayers, knowing that we were making the best decision for our family's future.

Upon our relocation to Texas and the subsequent settling in, we followed a familiar routine similar to our days in St. Augustine: enrolling our kids in school, acquainting ourselves with the community, and trying to find a church to call home. After a few months of exploration, we stumbled upon a church in a neighboring city that instantly resonated with us. One of their mottos—"No perfect people allowed"—struck a chord with our imperfect selves. As we became regular attendees, we found ourselves drawn to the warmth of the community, our children eagerly anticipating each visit, and I felt challenged to establish a daily connection with God. It was a spiritual discipline I had never truly embraced before. Though I had attended church sporadically throughout my life, committing to daily time with God was uncharted territory.

As I embarked on this newfound journey, God began to unveil profound truths to me through His Word—revelations I had never before conceived. The insights He imparted were so transformative that I felt compelled to share them with anyone who would listen. Then, on an ordinary weekday morning, I felt a divine nudge to turn to the book of Haggai. While perhaps familiar to some, I had never encountered this book before. Moreover, my engagement with the Old Testament had often been a struggle, so I was confused by God's leadership. Yet, as I delved into the words that God had tasked Haggai to convey to His people, I couldn't shake the feeling that God intended to impart a similar message to His people today—and that He was choosing me as the vessel for its delivery.

The book of Haggai in the NLT is printed just before chapter 1 to serve as a reference point throughout our journey together (in case you are like me and have never seen it before).

The Lord told Haggai to show His people that they were all living in fine houses while His Temple lay in ruins. He then showed them that the results they were getting in different areas of their lives were a direct result of not putting Him first and allowing His temple to be second to their own agendas.

I started to draw parallels between the behavior of the people of Jerusalem in ancient times, my actions, and those of the broader Western world. Many of us were consumed with building our own lives, neglecting to prioritize the construction of God's temple within us. As I pondered this concept, I realized that if God resides within us, then we are His temple. I had to confront whether I was truly nurturing this temple—physically, spiritually, emotionally, and mentally—or if I was too preoccupied with worldly pursuits and personal ambitions. This revelation hit me hard.

I spent a week immersing myself in the book, delving deeper into its relevance to my life. With each reading, I felt compelled to jot down the key insights I was receiving. Soon, I had thirteen main points scribbled down. Then came the title.

Initially, I couldn't understand why God would entrust me, an ordinary person with no significant platform or audience, with such profound insights into a two-chapter book of the Bible I had never explored before. It left me frustrated and questioning. When I asked God why He chose me for this task, His response was simple: I was to focus on what I had, not what I lacked. I might not have had the credentials or resources that society values, but I had a computer and

> I was to focus on what I had, not what I lacked.

a voice. Armed with just those two things, I began transcribing my thoughts into a Word document, following the guidance I believed the Lord had provided me.

Over a month, I transformed those thirteen points into thirteen chapters, each representing the wisdom I had gleaned during my contemplative moments on the porch. Though my writing was rough and in need of extensive editing, I was astounded to find that I had amassed around 30,000 words—a substantial amount considering the brevity of the source material, which contained just 926 words in the NLT version of the Bible. If that wasn't evidence of divine inspiration, then I didn't know what was.

During a quiet moment a couple of weeks later, while contemplating whether to make edits at that instant, I noticed an email notification on my phone. I typically overlook random emails—I mean, I have nearly 40,000 unread ones—but something about this one caught my eye, prompting me to open it. To my surprise, it was from TBN, a network I'd seen on television before. With curiosity piqued, I wondered why they were reaching out to me. It turned out to be a message from my current publisher, inquiring if I had ever considered publishing a book. I hadn't actively sought publishing opportunities or conducted any online searches about it; this endeavor was solely between God and me. I hadn't even disclosed to my wife the extent of my writing; she was only aware of my excitement about what God was revealing to me.

Feeling uncertain about my next steps, I turned to prayer for guidance. Should I even send this manuscript for publishing? After all, I wasn't some seasoned writer or renowned speaker—I was just an ordinary person. As I prayed, I happened to glance up at the sky and saw a striking "T" formed by plane trails. It might sound cliché, but it felt like a sign.

With a mix of nerves and excitement, I decided to take a leap of faith and send the first few chapters to TBN. I wasn't expecting much, to be honest. But then, about a week later, I received an email saying they wanted to publish my book. I was stunned. Yet, amidst the thrill came a wave of apprehension. This was a significant opportunity, and I couldn't shake the fear of somehow messing it all up.

Now that you've heard the story behind the creation of this book, it wasn't a calculated endeavor, nor was it a strategic move. This is about delivering a message that I believe God wants to reach someone who's been grappling with parts of their life that seem unfixable despite their best efforts.

Whether this book impacts one person or a million, my conviction remains: God desires His people to go on the journey of rebuilding the temple that is ourselves. After all, God resides within us. If we neglect the task of intentionally reconstructing His dwelling within us, we risk missing out on the incredible purpose that awaits us.

As Haggai teaches us, "Consider how things are going for you." Are you tirelessly attempting to fix something only to find it deteriorating further with each attempt? Do you pour more effort into fixing it, only to yield less than desired returns? Are you broken, trying to mask your struggles while knowing deep down that superficial fixes won't suffice?

If any of this resonates with you, as it does with parts of my own life, I invite you to join me on this journey as we commit to rebuilding God's temple. Let's embark on this endeavor with the understanding that by prioritizing the construction of His temple within us, we earn His trust to walk in our divine purpose to its fullest extent.

In His name and for His glory, let's rebuild together!

Haggai

On August 29 of the second year of King Darius's reign, the LORD gave a message through the prophet Haggai to Zerubbabel son of Shealtiel, governor of Judah, and to Jeshua son of Jehozadak, the high priest.

"This is what the LORD of Heaven's Armies says: The people are saying, 'The time has not yet come to rebuild the house of the LORD.'"

Then the LORD sent this message through the prophet Haggai: "Why are you living in luxurious houses while my house lies in ruins? This is what the LORD of Heaven's Armies says: Look at what's happening to you! You have planted much but harvest little. You eat but are not satisfied. You drink but are still thirsty. You put on clothes but cannot keep warm. Your wages disappear as though you were putting them in pockets filled with holes!

"This is what the LORD of Heaven's Armies says: Look at what's happening to you! Now go up into the hills, bring down timber, and rebuild my house. Then I will take pleasure in it and be honored, says the LORD.

You hoped for rich harvests, but they were poor. And when you brought your harvest home, I blew it away. Why? Because my house lies in ruins, says the LORD of Heaven's Armies, while all of you are busy building your own fine houses. It's because of you that the heavens withhold the dew and the earth produces no crops. I have called for a drought on your fields and hills—a drought to wither the grain and grapes and olive trees and all your other crops, a drought to starve you and your livestock and to ruin everything you have worked so hard to get."

Then Zerubbabel son of Shealtiel, and Jeshua son of Jehozadak, the high priest, and the whole remnant of God's people began to obey the message from the LORD their God. When they heard the words of the prophet Haggai, whom the LORD their God had sent, the people feared the LORD. Then Haggai, the LORD's messenger, gave the people this message from the LORD: "I am with you, says the LORD!"

So the LORD sparked the enthusiasm of Zerubbabel son of Shealtiel, governor of Judah, and the enthusiasm of Jeshua son of Jehozadak, the high priest, and the enthusiasm of the whole remnant of God's people. They began to work on the house of their God, the LORD of Heaven's Armies, on September 21 of the second year of King Darius's reign.

Then on October 17 of that same year, the LORD sent another message through the prophet Haggai. "Say this to Zerubbabel son of Shealtiel, governor of Judah, and to Jeshua son of Jehozadak, the high priest, and to the remnant of God's people there in the land: 'Does anyone remember this house—this Temple—in its former splendor? How, in comparison, does it look to you now? It must seem like nothing at all! But now the LORD says: Be strong, Zerubbabel. Be strong, Jeshua son of Jehozadak, the high priest. Be strong, all you people still left in the land. And now get to work, for I am with you, says the LORD of Heaven's Armies. My Spirit remains among you, just as I promised when you came out of Egypt. So do not be afraid.'

"For this is what the LORD of Heaven's Armies says: In just a little while I will again shake the heavens and the earth, the oceans and the dry land. I will shake all the nations, and the treasures of all the nations will be brought to this Temple. I will fill this place with glory, says the LORD of Heaven's Armies. The silver is mine, and the gold is mine, says the LORD of Heaven's Armies. The future glory of this Temple will be greater than its past glory, says the LORD of Heaven's Armies. And in this place I will bring peace. I, the LORD of Heaven's Armies, have spoken!"

On December 18 of the second year of King Darius's reign, the LORD sent this message to the prophet Haggai: "This is what the LORD of Heaven's Armies says. Ask the priests this question about the law: 'If one of you is carrying some meat from a holy sacrifice in his robes and his robe happens to brush against some bread or stew, wine or olive oil, or any other kind of food, will it also become holy?'"

The priests replied, "No."

Then Haggai asked, "If someone becomes ceremonially unclean by touching a dead person and then touches any of these foods, will the food be defiled?"

And the priests answered, "Yes."

Then Haggai responded, "That is how it is with this people and this nation, says the LORD. Everything they do and everything they offer is defiled by their sin. Look at what was happening to you before you began to lay the foundation of the LORD's Temple. When you hoped for a twenty-bushel crop, you harvested only ten. When you expected to draw fifty gallons from the winepress, you found only twenty. I sent blight and mildew and hail to destroy everything you worked so hard to produce. Even so, you refused to return to me, says the LORD.

"Think about this eighteenth day of December, the day when the foundation of the LORD's Temple was laid. Think carefully. I am giving you a promise now while the seed is still in the barn. You have not yet harvested your grain, and your grapevines, fig trees, pomegranates, and olive trees have not yet produced their crops. But from this day onward I will bless you."

On that same day, December 18, the LORD sent this second message to Haggai: "Tell Zerubbabel, the governor of Judah, that I am about to shake the heavens and the earth. I will overthrow royal thrones and destroy the power of foreign kingdoms. I will overturn their chariots and riders. The horses will fall, and their riders will kill each other.

"But when this happens, says the LORD of Heaven's Armies, I will honor you, Zerubbabel son of Shealtiel, my servant. I will make you like a signet ring on my finger, says the LORD, for I have chosen you. I, the LORD of Heaven's Armies, have spoken!

Haggai 1–2

Answering the Call

CHAPTER 1

The Limits of Repairing

Imagine you're cruising down the highway, enjoying the drive, when a car passes you on the left. It's a sleek black sedan, but something seems off. As it zooms past, you notice the side mirror looks a bit...jerry-rigged. As you look closer, yep, you guessed it—duct tape! The driver's gone all out, wrapping that mirror up like a mummy. You can't help but chuckle nervously, hoping it holds on tight.

The first time I remember seeing something like this as a driving adult was exactly like this, and I remember what I asked myself. It was a sunny day, cruising down I-95 in Orlando, Florida, when I spotted a car with a patchwork of duct tape. Layers upon layers held together the windshield, the side window, and a dangling piece of the side mirror. It had taken a beating. Yet, instead of a proper fix, someone had resorted to the trusty old duct tape solution. As I trailed behind, wary of any sudden movements, I couldn't help but wonder wouldn't it be simpler just to rebuild that part of the car?

Maybe it was easier. Maybe they didn't have time. Maybe they didn't have or want to spend the money. There could have been a lot of possible reasons, I guess. But I knew one thing: there was no way anyone could want the result of the duct tape job I saw on their car, forever.

We have all seen things like this, where the repair job was half-baked at best, and while the intent is to "do it right at a later date," it stays in that kind of fixed space for another week. Then another two weeks. Then that turns into a month. Then, before we know it, we are living with this cheap fix for a whole year. We have kind of gotten used to it.

Sometimes, we're just like that car on the highway, resorting to quick fixes and temporary solutions to mask the cracks in our lives. We plaster smiles on our faces, dress up, and head to church, hoping to conceal our struggles. We camouflage our problems with carefully curated social media posts or drown them in more damaging fixes like alcohol, porn, or gambling. We numb ourselves with binge-watching Netflix or indulging in excessive online shopping. These makeshift solutions become the shaky foundations upon which we build our lives. It's easier to cover them up than to confront them head-on, dig deep, and rebuild on a stronger foundation.

See, the truth is that repairing doesn't work for long because it only hides the root cause. Repairing also doesn't work because that is not the genesis of how God works. See, in 2 Corinthians 5:17, it says, "...anyone who belongs to Christ has become a new person. The old life is gone; a new life has begun!"

> *Anyone who belongs to Christ has become a new person. The old life is gone; a new life has begun!*
> 2 Corinthians 5:17

What it does not say is, "Those who become Christians are fixed. We're going to fix the stuff that's in them." That's not what it says. It says we are a whole new person. We're not even the same creation. The old creation is gone forever. And a brand-new creation is here. God is not fixing things. He's completely making us new.

So, if God plans to rebuild us, it makes me wonder if a quick fix within ourselves is the right long-term strategy. The beginning of our journey is to decide whether or not rebuilding something is actually needed based on our situations in the first place. I mean, sometimes, a simple fix works. If that's the case, fantastic. Simple maintenance can work if we have the foundation and structures that we need to fulfill the purpose God has for us. It can also work if the challenges we're having aren't consistent or don't hurt you, others, or the future purpose of either of those two parties. But there are also times when we think fixing will work, and it seems that every time we try and fix things, it only leads to more problems. It can be tricky to figure out when repairing will do the trick or if a rebuild is what is needed in an area of our lives. While asking God what to do is the first thing we should do, there are also other factors you can consider. Here are some considerations to help determine if a quick fix will do the trick.

1. Extent of the damage: Assess the extent of the damage. If the issues are minor and can be resolved with simple fixes, then repairing might be the best option. However, if the damage is extensive and affects the core structure, rebuilding may be necessary. Lamentations 3:40 (NIV) encourages us to "examine our ways and test them, and let us return to the Lord."
2. Frequency of problems: Consider how often the issues occur. If you find yourself repeatedly fixing the same problem, it may be a sign that a

more comprehensive rebuilding process is needed. Often, frequency will lead to severity.

3. Long-term goals: Reflect on your long-term goals and aspirations. If fixing aligns with your immediate needs but not your future vision, rebuilding might be the more strategic choice. Philippians 3:13–14 encourages us to forget what is behind and strain toward what is ahead, pressing on toward the goal of winning the prize for which God has called us heavenward in Christ Jesus.

> Often, frequency will lead to severity.

4. Resources and time: Luke 14:28–30 highlights the importance of planning and counting the cost before starting a significant project. Evaluate the resources and time available to you. While rebuilding requires more investment upfront, it can save time and resources in the long run by preventing recurring issues. And always remember that if God is asking you to rebuild yourself or a part of you, He will fill in the gap of any resources you may not have naturally. If we lean on Him, he will provide what we need to do what He is asking of us.

Lesson One of Many from the Escalade

Back in 2007, at the ripe age of twenty, I was dead set on getting myself a shiny new car. But not just any car—a brand-spanking-new 2007 Cadillac Escalade EXT! Looking back, it's easy to see now how misguided my financial decisions were, but back then, I was convinced I was making the right move. I mean, I was pulling in around $2500 a month waiting tables at the restaurant, and with rent only costing me $300 a month split between three roommates, I figured I had plenty of cash to spare. So, armed with some salesmanship and a willing co-signer in the form of my dad, I drove off the lot in my dream car. The smell of the leather, the envy-inducing stares as I cruised down the road—it was all worth it, or so I thought.

Then reality hit. With a monthly car payment of $1100 and insurance ringing in at another $400 a month, my dream ride was quickly turning into a financial nightmare. Before I knew it, I was shelling out $1500 a month before even factoring in gas—which, by the way, was skyrocketing to over $4 a gallon for the first time in Florida. Panic set in as I scrambled to make ends meet, picking up extra shifts and even resorting to putting my car payment on a forgotten Macy's credit card I'd received when I turned eighteen. Not my finest moment, I'll admit.

But when that well ran dry, and I found myself drowning in debt, I had to swallow my pride and make a desperate call to my grandmother, begging her for a loan to help cover my payments. It was a humbling moment—one that left me feeling utterly ashamed sitting in my apartment room crying out of shame. In less than a year, I'd managed to dig myself into a $30,000 hole with a truck I could barely afford, tacking on another $5,000 in credit card debt just to keep up appearances. Something had to change, and fast.

You see, I had been trying to repair my financial situation that whole year, all because of the stupidity I displayed by purchasing the truck in the first place. When one band-aid didn't work, I tried another one. When one thing fell through, I tried to cover it up with another fix. I mean, what were my options? My whole identity was wrapped up in this truck. I was the guy who "had money." I was the guy who "had it figured out" before anyone else. I was the guy who "had no stress." I was the guy who had the answers to make my life a success at such an early age. What would happen if people figured out that I wasn't any of those things? Would they stop being my friend? Would they feel betrayed? Would they leave?

While this was one of the most painful parts of my life, I am very grateful that it happened so early on because it taught me one of the most valuable lessons I've ever learned.

I wish I could say that the year I had to sell the truck taught me all I needed to know and that I rebuilt my identity on more solid ground and moved forward with a life built on faith and truth. But that's not how it played out. Yes, I sold the truck, but instead of facing the need to rebuild that part of my life, I chose to hide behind lies and deception. I made up a story and did everything to maintain the facade of having it all together. It was just another attempt to patch things up.

Repairing, however, only added more unnecessary stress to my life. Have you ever tried to fix something and thought, "That should do it"? Every time you use that thing, open that door, or sit on that chair, there's a nagging doubt: "I hope it holds up. I hope it doesn't collapse. I hope it doesn't break again." Deep down, we know that fixing things instead of rebuilding them is just a shortcut. When I was focused on fixing my financial problems, all I cared about was avoiding getting caught and not truly rebuilding for a stable future.

Often, the same thing happens when we do that within ourselves. We know that we took the shortcut. Subconsciously, we know that we didn't do the full work. And so, as soon as a storm of life comes, there is an extra level of anxiety that is unnecessarily there because we took the shortcut.

I don't know about you, but there is enough anxiety and stress in life to not add any more to myself. I want to do everything I can to reduce the level of stress, worry, and anxiousness around me. So, if that means I need to do more work than most to rebuild versus repair, that's the route that I became willing to go to avoid that extra stress. While the temptation to repair may be there, there are also limitations to taking that route that we will experience. Below are just a few.

> There is enough anxiety and stress in life to not add any more to myself.

Superficial Solutions

Fixing often addresses only the surface issues without tackling the root causes. For instance, patching up a recurring conflict in a relationship without understanding and resolving the underlying issues will likely result in the problem resurfacing. Proverbs 28:13 (NIV) reminds us: "Whoever conceals their sins does not prosper, but the one who confesses and renounces them finds mercy." The freedom we can experience while rebuilding is only available when we do the work to go deep. The work isn't necessarily physical. A lot of times, it can be increasing our vulnerability in an area we're trying to rebuild and allowing others to realize we're not perfect, and in that area, we know we need to go deeper. The only way we get to experience grace is when we need it and are honest about the need for it to God, ourselves, and others. Not only do we get to experience deeper healing when we rebuild, but we also give others permission to expose an area in their life they need to rebuild to someone and

> *Whoever conceals their sins does not prosper, but the one who confesses and renounces them finds mercy.*
> Proverbs 28:13

begin the work within themselves they may be holding back out of guilt or shame. Avoiding the superficial solution and allowing God to help us rebuild has so many benefits.

Temporary Relief

Fixing can provide a temporary solution but may not offer long-term stability. Over time, the same issues may recur, requiring repeated fixes. This can be exhausting and frustrating, leading to a sense of stagnation. Jesus highlighted this principle in Matthew 9:16–17, where He talked about putting new wine into old wineskins and the inevitable failure of such a temporary fix. This is tough, too, because we live in a time where many of the world's solutions are temporary. We're all about getting a version of a fix that is quick, cost-effective, and takes the least amount of effort or thought. While it feels like it worked initially, the time comes when the band-aid comes off and the scar is exposed that we should've dealt with differently to heal completely, and we are forced to choose how to deal with that area again. This is tough to do over and over, and the time it takes to solve the same things continually may cause us to miss something God would have us do that would bring us to a new level—all because we need to fix the temporary nature of our past decision to repair, instead of rebuild in an area.

> In some cases, what appears to be a fix can compromise the integrity of the original structure.

Structural Weakness

In some cases, what appears to be a fix can compromise the integrity of the original structure. For example, continually repairing a leaky roof without addressing the fundamental issues of the roofing structure can lead to more significant damage over time. Jesus' parable of the wise and foolish builders in Matthew 7:24–

27 emphasizes the importance of building on a solid foundation. While fixing this on the surface can seem like it's going well if our foundation can't support the fix, even if the repair is "done well," the foundation's weakness comes out in the end. We will touch on this in chapter 5, and the foundational ability we will carry with a rebuild is far superior to not dealing with the foundation of an issue. When both the foundation and the structure that is showing are broken in an area in our life, even rebuilding the structure leaves out a very important component in the foundation. Structural fixes without foundational strength may last a bit longer than other repairs, but eventually, they still leave us exposed to damage.

We get encouragement from God's word for times when we rebuild, though, as shown when God tells His people in Haggai 2:4 (NIV) to take courage "and work, for I am with you." The comfort of knowing we get to rely on His strength throughout the process, knowing we are following His guidance, is immensely helpful.

It is also encouraging to know that if you're willing to do the rebuilding instead of taking the shortcut of repairing, you will live a life of fruitfulness that most may not experience. Rebuilding something is hard. Most people are not willing to do it. That's why many aspects of the world often feel fragile, like they're just barely holding together. The more we opt for quick fixes instead of genuine rebuilding, the more vulnerable everything becomes to falling apart when challenges arise.

The US economy in 2023 is a great macro example. Over the years, we've often resorted to temporary fixes instead of addressing underlying economic issues. As a result, our national debt has reached $33 trillion, creating a significant challenge for the future. While we've been delaying the inevitable, it's important to recognize that, eventually, we'll need to address these issues and rebuild our economic foundation. The longer we wait to do so, the more challenging it will be to create a new foundation for the future.

The same is true of you and me. Now, you may be thinking, *I wish I would have rebuilt myself with a new foundation earlier. It's a little late in my life now.* The good news is you're never going to be younger than you are today. Today's a good day to start. Today is a good day to decide, "I'm tired of trying to fix everything in my life and trying to make it look like it's built properly. Everything that I'm trying to fix is a byproduct of the foundation and the structure that's currently built in and around me. Perhaps it's time for me to do the work of the rebuild and stop trying to fix everything."

> You're never going to be younger than you are today. Today is a good day to start.

Also, know that everything we are building or rebuilding now will be passed on. Whether to the next generation or to others you come in contact with, whether employees, friends, neighbors, or acquaintances. Everything we do, everything we become, has an impact on people. So whether you're twenty-five or seventy-five, doing the work to rebuild an area of yourself will not go unnoticed. It will not return void. It will affect you and the people you touch, and your Father in heaven will see and know that you had the heart and desire to rebuild His temple. God smiles when we prioritize Him, and we are lucky enough that He gives us the ability to enjoy the benefits of this decision along the way.

If you're prepared to move beyond quick fixes and embrace the process of rebuilding, then let's roll up our sleeves and get started!

CHAPTER 2

Rebuilding versus Repairing

What's the Difference?

As a corporate leader, I've faced numerous challenges in revitalizing struggling sales teams throughout my career. Each time I stepped into a new role, I was confronted with a critical decision: should I patch up the existing structure to improve performance or embark on a complete reconstruction from the ground up? This pivotal choice, though recurring, was never easy, as the stakes were high and time was of the essence in the fast-paced world of Corporate America.

In the business world, just as in everything else, rebuilding means laying a new foundation; typically, that foundation lies in the people. Did we have the right foundation? Did we have the right belief system? Did we have a foundation strong enough not only to support the first-year or second-year performance, but also growth over a sustained amount of time? That was how I was introduced to this concept.

As you think about scenarios in your life where you have taken a shortcut or added a temporary fix, the rest of this book is going to challenge your future decisions on whether rebuilding is an option from the onset of a problem or challenge and how to recognize and seize the opportunity. While rebuilding things can apply to business, relationships, or marriages, this book will focus on rebuilding yourself.

The Bible says we are the house of God, and He lives in us, so it is critical to pay attention to when God references "His temple" throughout the text. In the Old Testament, He was referring to His actual temple. When King Solomon built God's temple, it was a physical building. When the Bible mentions it in books like Ezra, Haggai, and Zechariah, it refers to the actual building.

As we stand today, we are His temple. Every one of us. The Bible makes it clear in 1 Corinthians 3:16: "Don't you realize that all of you together are the temple of God and that the Spirit of God lives in you?" This is incredible! The spirit of the Creator of the universe, who put the stars in the sky, who tells the oceans where to stop, who knows the end from the beginning, and who will be the Alpha and Omega for all eternity, lives inside of you! Let's pause here and take the time to meditate and think on this and the amazing reality of it before going

The spirit of the Creator of the universe, who put the stars in the sky, who tells the oceans where to stop, who knows the end from the beginning, and who will be the Alpha and the Omega for all eternity, lives inside of you!

on to the rest of this chapter. When we get a deeper revelation of this, it may offer us a perspective and inspire us to the importance of rebuilding ourselves, if not for that fact alone.

Since we are the temple of God, let's figure out what God says about whether we should be rebuilding ourselves or not. He gives us amazing clarity in the small but powerful book of Haggai. Look at what He says to pay attention to in chapter 1:5-6: "Look at what's happening to you! You have planted much but harvested little. You eat but are not satisfied. You drink but are still thirsty. You put on clothes but cannot keep warm. Your wages disappear as though you were putting them in pockets filled with holes!" Let's dig in and see if these things are happening broadly today.

1. Obesity rates: In 2023, nearly 42 percent of US adults were grappling with obesity, a staggering statistic that mirrors the pervasive issue of excess in our modern world. This epidemic of overconsumption is reminiscent of the spiritual famine described in the book of Haggai. The prophet Haggai admonished the people for focusing on their own desires and neglecting their spiritual nourishment. Similarly, our obsession with indulgence and instant gratification leaves us spiritually malnourished, despite our physi-

cal abundance. We're eating, but we're not truly satisfied.

2. Financial struggles: The data from bankrate.com paints a grim picture of financial instability. A majority of adults are living paycheck to paycheck, regardless of their income bracket. This reflects a pattern of financial mismanagement and lack of foresight, akin to the negligence highlighted in Haggai's prophecy. The people were urged to prioritize the rebuilding of God's temple, yet they focused on their comforts and neglected their spiritual responsibilities. Similarly, our preoccupation with materialism and immediate pleasures leads to financial bondage, leaving us enslaved to debt and devoid of financial freedom. Sounds like a parallel to wages disappearing as if put in pockets filled with holes, if you ask me.

3. Stagnant wage growth: Despite advancements in technology and economic growth, the median household income in the US hasn't seen significant improvement over the years. In fact, when adjusted for inflation, it might seem like wages are disappearing into thin air, much like coins slipping through pockets filled with holes. This echoes the sentiments expressed in Haggai, where the people worked tirelessly but saw little

fruit from their labor. They sowed much but harvested little—a consequence of their misplaced priorities and lack of alignment with God's will. Similarly, our relentless pursuit of wealth and worldly success often leads to disillusionment when we realize that true fulfillment cannot be found in material possessions. Planting much but harvesting little isn't fun, whether in Haggai's time or now.

In essence, these data points serve as sobering reminders of the consequences of neglecting spiritual nourishment and prioritizing temporal pleasures over eternal values. Like the people in the time of Haggai, we are called to reassess our priorities, seek first the kingdom of God, and trust in His provision for our needs. Only then can we break free from the cycle of excess and find true satisfaction in Him.

While it is obvious to those of us willing to pay attention that we need to rebuild some key areas, a quick fix has become the norm. Fixing things takes less time and less energy, and it often gives off the look and feel of a completely new person, new attitude, or new habit. The challenge is that we need sustained change. Remember the duct-taped side mirror? We all know it is just a matter of time before it comes flying off and bounces down the road.

The other side that nobody wants to talk about is that when we rebuild something, we must first tear down the current structure. If I simply build a new structure on top of the current one, that's going to be one funny-looking house. It would also have a flimsy foundation that, over time, would wear down and create instability, likely costing more investment of added resources to fix long term. Tearing down takes time and vulnerability, two things we aren't too fond of in today's world. The benefits, however, are many, and here are just a few we see, with Scripture as our guide.

Rebuilding, on the other hand, involves starting from scratch to create something new and stronger. It requires more time, effort, and resources but offers profound benefits, such as the following.

Addressing Root Causes

Rebuilding allows you to examine the foundational issues that caused the problems in the first place. By addressing these root causes, you create a more robust and resilient structure that can withstand future challenges. Isaiah 58:12 (NIV) says, "Your people will rebuild the ancient ruins and will raise up the age-old foundations; you will be called Repairer of Broken Walls, Restorer of Streets with Dwellings." Knowing our foundations have been dealt with allows us to walk in true freedom. It's like walking into your boss' office knowing you have truly done your work well, with integrity and diligence each day you've worked there. It doesn't mean our boss may not bring problems to us or ask us to do things differently, but foundationally, I have nothing to hide. I don't have to wonder if they caught me doing something that was a quick-fix version of my work. I know I have done everything thoroughly and honestly, and whatever that conversation leads to, good or bad, I know the root of my work is good. That freedom is something we can't put a price on.

Long-Term Stability

Rebuilding provides an opportunity to create lasting solutions. For instance, rebuilding a broken trust in a relationship through consistent actions and open communication can lead to a stronger bond that is less likely to break under pressure. In Jeremiah 24:6 (NIV),

> Rebuilding provides an opportunity to create lasting solutions.

God promises, "My eyes will watch over them for their good, and I will bring them back to this land. I will build them up and not tear them down; I will plant them and not uproot them." If I shatter a pot, I can't repair it to be the same pot again. There has been too much damage to the structure. But if I decide to rebuild, with new intent, and a better understanding of what the future of it can be, I can make a mosaic by simply putting in effort, creativity, and willingness to create something new. The value of that rebuild is often far more valuable than the original thing. And the same is true in a lot of areas of our lives. Whether relationships, habits, family, or whatever other areas may be shattered, being willing to rebuild into a new, more honest, more purpose-driven version creates the long-term stability we all desire.

Improved Functionality

Starting anew allows for the incorporation of improvements and advancements that were not part of the original structure. Whether it's updating a skill set, adopting healthier habits, or integrating new technologies, rebuilding can lead to enhanced performance and greater satisfaction. As 2 Corinthians 5:17 (NIV) tells us, "Therefore, if anyone is in Christ, the new creation has come: The old has gone, the new is here!" As we talked about in the last chapter, the keyword is new. It's not fixed. A rebuilt temple of God doesn't mean we forget where we've come from, or what we used to be. It just means we know that what we used to be won't allow for our

> The keyword is new. It's not fixed.

purpose to be fulfilled, and we're willing to do the work to allow God to work through us and trust us more. The functionality of making these decisions will be both practical and peaceful. It takes much less effort to make advancements in an area, too, knowing the foundation and structure of our new selves can handle those advancements toward the next level.

Renewed Vision

Rebuilding often comes with a fresh perspective and a renewed sense of purpose. It allows you to redefine goals, set new standards, and create a vision that aligns more closely with your values and aspirations. Proverbs 29:18 (KJV) states, "Where there is no vision, the people perish," highlighting the importance of a clear, renewed vision. While I have often defined perish as immediate, I wonder if it may indicate a slow degradation of ourselves in an area due to continual quick fixes. I wonder if we're perishing almost without realizing it. The ability to get a fresh, new vision due to our willingness to rebuild ourselves in areas often has multiplying effects. When I rebuild, it allows God to show me new and different paths He would like to take me on. Knowing that, because I have rebuilt His temple in the areas He highlighted to me, He can trust me to go on journeys not otherwise seen based on my old version of that area. New vision equals new excitement. See, who said this had to be a completely boring process?

> New vision equals new excitement.

Let's delve deeper into the concept of rebuilding in the coming chapters. We'll explore the breaking down, the building up, and the amazing future we have in store when we put God's temple first. We'll take a close look at the current foundation of our lives and the factors that have shaped it. What led us to this point, and how could rebuilding pave the way for the transformation we yearn for?

This book is going to be about you and me and how we can rebuild ourselves. This book is going to be about how rebuilding is worth it. Yes, it takes more time. Yes, it takes more energy. And yes, it takes more resources. However, the only way to create sustainable and lasting change on a foundation that can hold up over tough years, tough relationships, and the trials that Jesus promises we will go through is to rebuild the areas of our life where it's needed.

In this book, we'll tackle important topics that show why rebuilding is a worthwhile endeavor. We'll then move into actionable steps to guide you through the process. I've broken it down into five key components with detailed subsections to make it practical and manageable. We'll start by examining how you're currently built and the foundation you're standing on. Remember, prioritizing yourself is crucial because you can't pour from an empty cup. We'll discuss the process of dismantling the old structure, tearing up the worn-out foundation, and laying down a sturdy new one. And finally, we'll address some of the challenges that come with rebuilding, acknowledging that it's not always easy but emphasizing the importance of persevering through the journey.

Let's be clear from the start: there will be challenges ahead. When we face obstacles, discouragement, or resistance from others, it's all part of the journey. It doesn't mean we're on the wrong path. We must remember that enduring change requires effort, but the results will be worth it. As we embark on this journey, we'll need support from others and a clear understanding of the tools and resources available to us. Together, we'll build something stronger, healthier, and more vibrant than what exists today.

This is going to be a journey, but it's going to be a journey worth taking. Here is my first encouragement of many throughout our time together: while rebuilding takes more time than repairing, it takes less time than you think if you commit to the process.

I'm excited to go on this journey with you. I'm excited to dive into some of the thought processes and the stories that have been brought to me and that I've learned as I've dug into this work. Being able to get honest, open, and transparent about the fact that our repairs are starting to fail us is the first step for keeping the whole structure from crashing down.

This could mean a physical challenge to you. This could mean a mental challenge to you. This can be an emotional challenge to you. Maybe all of the above. This may be a stretch in ways that you may not have been stretched before and, hopefully, it will help you think about things in a slightly different light than you have in the past. If we want lasting change as people, as parents, as neighbors, as community members, as employers, as employees, as people striving for greatness, as people striving to live out our God-given purpose, sometimes we have to be willing to get down to the foundation and be willing to start anew.

We're going to do this together. One step at a time. The first thing we're going to look at is what our current structure looks like.

Let's dive in!

Breaking Down

CHAPTER 3

Your Current Structure

In our journey toward rebuilding, it's essential to understand the structure upon which our lives are built. Just as a builder assesses the condition of a house before renovations, we must examine the habits, associations, thoughts, and words that shape our daily lives. Without this critical evaluation, any efforts to improve or transform will be superficial at best, leaving us vulnerable to future setbacks.

Imagine a house with old beams beginning to rot or split. No matter how beautifully you paint the walls or how exquisitely you furnish the rooms, the underlying structural issues will eventually cause problems. Similarly, if we neglect to examine and address the core elements of our lives—our habits, associations, thoughts, and words—we risk undermining our progress and potential for lasting change.

Evaluating with Intention

As we begin this chapter on evaluating the fundamental aspects of our lives, it is crucial to approach the process with intention and honesty. Each element has a vital role in shaping our spiritual and emotional well-being. By examining and realigning these areas with biblical principles, we enable ourselves to see which pieces of these elements can remain and which pieces need to be rebuilt to support the future we desire.

In the following sections, we will delve deeper into each of these critical components, providing practical guidance and scriptural insights to help you with this evaluation. Through this journey, we can ensure that our transformation is both profound and enduring, leading to a life of greater fulfillment and alignment with God's will.

Habits

Our current structure is often shaped by the habits and patterns we've developed over time. These habits can be both positive and negative, influencing every aspect of our lives. In Romans 12:2 (NIV), Paul writes, "Do not conform to the pattern of this world, but be transformed by the renewing of your mind. Then you will be able to test and approve what God's will is—his good, pleasing and perfect will." This verse encourages us to break free from negative patterns and align our lives with God's will. Studies have shown that approximately 40 percent of our daily actions come from habits we have built over time. We don't think about them. We don't even consider if they're still good things to do or not. We simply do what our habit tells us to do and reap the consequence of it, often unconsciously.

> Our current structure is often shaped by the habits and patterns we have developed over time.

This is a great place to start to look at when beginning, as it's simple to take inventory of your habits. Simply sit down, think about as many things that you do that are automatic, and write them down. Then, do a quick, honest evaluation of whether that habit is helpful or hurtful to your desired state in the area you're trying to rebuild. And yes, those are the only two options: helpful or hurtful. Sometimes, we think that something we do has no effect

> We're either going toward a desired state or away from it, even if it's so small it's hard to notice.

when, in reality, we are never stagnant. We're either going toward a desired state or away from it, even if it's so small it's hard to notice. We will cover some practical ways how to change any habits you need to a little later in the chapter, but having the habits you want to keep and those you want to change in an area you're rebuilding is a good starting point to begin to do the work to rebuild.

Associations

The people we surround ourselves with significantly impact our lives. Proverbs 13:20 (NIV) warns, "Walk with the wise and become wise, for a companion of fools suffers harm." Our associations can either uplift us and draw us closer to God, or they can lead us astray and weaken our spiritual foundation. It's essential to evaluate whether our relationships encourage growth, wisdom, and righteousness. Also, we may have relationships that have been amazing based on where we were in the past. They were friends or coworkers that we made great memories with and their relationships helped grow us in a season. And sometimes, seasons change. Some associations may have worked for where you were but won't work for where you're trying to go. These are tough to navigate. You may still love these people and want to see the best for them, and it can be hard to begin to evaluate their impact on your life.

However, this can be critical to our ability to rebuild ourselves and prioritize God where we need to. If people aren't bringing me up, they are, by default, bringing me down. Similar to the comment about habits, there is no such thing as neutral.

Sometimes, our associations may not be toxic, which is obviously bad, but they may be complacent, which is sneakily bad. Nothing obvious is wrong, but there is a slow drip of apathy toward the average that may be draining us of the strength in our structure that we need to fulfill our destiny. Our evaluation of our associations can be tough because people we probably care for are involved, but if we decide to rebuild our structure, knowing which pieces can stay and which can go, and being honest about that, is going to be critical.

> Sometimes, our associations may be toxic, which is obviously bad, but they may be complacent, which is sneakily bad.

Thoughts

Our thoughts shape our identity and actions. Proverbs 23:7a (NKJV) says, "For as he thinks in his heart, so is he." Negative thoughts rooted in fear, doubt, or insecurity can hinder our rebuilding efforts. Romans 12:2 (NIV) encourages us, "Do not conform to the pattern of this world, but be transformed by the renewing of your mind." Renewing our minds with God's truth is crucial for transformation.

The simplest way to evaluate our thought life is to slow down. Asking ourselves several times a day why we are thinking about a situation, person, or interaction a certain way can offer insight into the areas of our thought life we may need to dig deeper into as we figure out which parts of our thoughts are conducive to staying during our rebuild, and which ones need to be dealt with.

Words

Our words have the power to build up or tear down. Proverbs 18:21 (NIV) teaches, "The tongue has the power of life and death, and those who love it will eat its fruit." The words we speak reflect the condition of our hearts and influence our reality. Jesus reminds us in Matthew 12:34b (NIV),

> The words we speak reflect the condition of our hearts and influence our reality.

"For the mouth speaks what the heart is full of." Therefore, it's important to align our speech with God's desired state for the area we're trying to rebuild. Do we build ourselves or others up or down? Which comments do we make to ourselves or others that are more full of doubt or fear than grace and hope? Sometimes, it's hard to control this one, as we are often quick to fly off the handle with empty or hurtful words, but examining how our words align with our purpose will allow us to find out if we are helping ourselves or hindering ourselves simply by the power of the words we're speaking.

What Can We Learn from Sarah?

One of my very close friends is an unbelievable example of this. For the sake of privacy, we will call her "Sarah." Sarah lived a life of constant busyness and chaos. She prided herself on her ability to juggle multiple responsibilities, but deep down, she felt a sense of emptiness and dissatisfaction.

One day, during a quiet moment of reflection, Sarah felt a stirring in her heart. She sensed that God was calling her to a deeper, more purposeful life. As she sought guidance through prayer and meditation on Scripture, Sarah began to realize that many of her daily habits and routines were hindering her from fulfilling God's purpose for her. They weren't aligned with who she wanted to be.

With a newfound determination, Sarah decided to embark on a journey of self-discovery and transformation. She turned to the Bible for wisdom and guidance, seeking out passages that spoke to the importance of living a life aligned with God's will.

As Sarah examined her current habits and routines in the light of Scripture, she was struck by how many of them were driven by worldly values rather than God's truth. She realized that she had been seeking fulfillment and validation in all the wrong places, neglecting her relationship with God in the process.

With God's help, Sarah began to make changes in her life. She started prioritizing time spent in prayer and meditation, seeking God's guidance in all areas of her life. She also learned to let go of the need for constant busyness and productivity, trusting in God's provision and timing instead.

As Sarah embraced God's purpose for her life, she experienced a profound transformation. She discovered a deep sense of peace and fulfillment that she had never known before. She found joy in serving others and sharing God's love with those around her.

Sarah's journey serves as a powerful reminder that true fulfillment can only be found in living a life that is aligned with God's purposes. By rebuilding herself according to God's plan, Sarah discovered a life of purpose, meaning, and abundance that far surpassed anything she could have imagined.

Identifying the pieces of our current structure that need rebuilding is a crucial step in the journey toward transformation. Here are some practical and applicable ways to accomplish this.

Self-Reflection

Set aside dedicated time for self-reflection. Journaling can be a helpful tool to record your thoughts, feelings, and observations about your daily habits, beliefs, and actions. Reflect on patterns of behavior that may be holding you back or causing distress in your life that may need to be rebuilt. Psalm 139:23–24 (NIV) shows us to invite God into these times by saying, "Search me, God, and know my heart; test me and know my anxious thoughts. See if there is any offensive way in me, and lead me in the way everlasting." This verse emphasizes the importance of inviting God into the process of self-examination, seeking His guidance to reveal areas needing change.

Seek Feedback

Ask trusted friends, family members, or mentors for feedback on your strengths and areas for growth. Their perspective can offer valuable insights into blind spots or patterns you may not have noticed on your own. While this takes courage and vulnerability, the wisdom and real insight gained is priceless. Proverbs 15:22

(NIV) tells us, "Plans fail for lack of counsel, but with many advisers they succeed." Seeking the wisdom and perspective of others can provide clarity and direction when considering rebuilding an area of our lives that we wouldn't be able to see by ourselves.

We often are cautious to do this, as it is naturally kind of scary. Putting ourselves out there to potentially (and if people are honest, probably) receive feedback that highlights part of ourselves we don't want to face can be intimidating. It can feel like we're getting criticized, and it can hurt. However, looking at it through the lens of voluntarily seeking insight we couldn't otherwise see may help us reduce the amount of personalization we apply to the hurt and allow us to address the behavior the other person is pointing out without being self-critical and believing it means we are a bad person. When we seek feedback from trusted people and allow ourselves to be vulnerable to get a pulse on what parts of our structure need addressing, we will be able to do a more complete work when rebuilding what is needed.

Review Past Experiences

Reflect on significant events or experiences in your life and consider how they have shaped your beliefs and behaviors. Are there unresolved issues or past traumas that continue to impact your present circumstances? Acknowledging and addressing these experiences can be a crucial step in the rebuilding process. Sometimes, it will be events that happened in childhood that led to a long period of shaped behavior that will need to be deeper explored, and others, we can find certain times in the recent past where we have noticed how the result of a behavior led to a result that wasn't good. Either way, it is worth digging into our past experiences to know what the cause and effect of our experiences have been so we can learn from them. Then, we can also identify if there are things that need to be dealt with when tearing down certain parts of our current structure to make room for a more sturdy one to support your future.

Evaluate Your Relationships

Assess the quality of your relationships and how they contribute to your overall well-being. Are there toxic or unhealthy dynamics in your relationships that need to be addressed? Consider how your interactions with others influence your thoughts and actions. "Do not be misled: 'Bad company corrupts good character'" (1 Corinthians 15:33, NIV). This verse highlights the importance of surrounding ourselves with positive influences

> *Do not be misled: bad company corrupts good character.*
> 1 Corinthians 15:33

and nurturing healthy relationships. If this is an area of contention, it may be a space that needs to be rebuilt, or it may even be a piece of rebuilding ourselves that will be key.

Author and speaker Jim Rohn highlighted this when he said, "You are the average of the five people you spend the most time with." Who are those people for you today? Evaluate as many aspects as you can. What are their beliefs? What are their habits? How do they talk, positively or negatively? How good is their marriage or relationship with their kids? All of these pieces and more. Then ask yourself, "Does this person and the life they live align with the life I want to live once I rebuild myself in an area?" If so, great! If not, it may be worth evaluating whether or not to keep them as close while you're in your rebuilding process. It doesn't necessarily mean they're bad people. It just may mean that their season to be in a close relationship with you may be coming to an end to ensure you have the right people around you for you to rebuild into the person you were created to be. It's not easy, but it's a piece of our structure that needs to be looked at to

> "You are the average of the five people you spend the most time with."
> Jim Rohn

see which relationships, if any, need to be eliminated or adjusted to ensure we have the right ones in place to get where we're trying to go.

Assess Your Thought Patterns

Think about what you think about. Pay attention to your thought patterns and the narratives you tell yourself. Are you prone to negative self-talk or limiting beliefs? Challenge these thought patterns and replace them with more empowering and positive affirmations. Romans 12:2 reminds us, "Don't copy the behavior and customs of the world, but let God transform you into a new person by changing the way you think." This encourages us to invite and allow God to renew our minds with positive and godly thoughts. It is said that people have about 60,000 thoughts each day. I would venture to say that most go without inspection. When we think about what we're thinking about, it allows us to insert more intention in our thought life which will lead to making better decisions. If, when we assess our thought patterns, we identify they're negative, critical, pessimistic, or even just apathetic, it may be worth digging into why and figuring out if we need to be more intentional when situations arise in our day-to-day lives. A lot of the thoughts I naturally had were ones I needed to tear down and look at the foundation of these so I could make more room for ones that better align with our desired future.

Consider Your Values and Priorities

Reflect on your values and priorities in life. Are you living in alignment with these values, or are there areas where you feel disconnected or unfulfilled? Clarifying your values can help guide your decisions and actions moving forward. "But seek first his kingdom and his righteousness, and all these things will be given to you as well," is what Jesus would tell us (Matthew 6:33, NIV). Prioritizing God's kingdom helps us align our values and actions with His will.

So many people don't know what their values and priorities really are, so beginning with identifying what these are is a critical step and one that most people fail to take. When once interviewed, Oprah Winfrey was asked what the one common trait of all the successful people was that she had interviewed over the years. Her answer was, "They all know what they want. They are crystal clear on what they want and where they are going." She noted that most people don't know what they want. We may know what we're trying to avoid, like poverty, trouble, or pain. We may also know what we want vaguely, like happiness, freedom, or love. But when we get crystal clear on the values and priorities we desire, we will have a higher probability of actually getting there. Furthermore, we will have an increased ability to identify when our thoughts, actions, words, or associations don't align with these values and priorities and can adjust more quickly.

Seek Professional Guidance

Consider seeking support from a counselor, therapist, or life coach who can provide professional guidance and support in the process of self-discovery and rebuilding. They can offer tools and strategies tailored to your unique needs and circumstances, and finding one who is aligned with your faith and values can also ensure biblical alignment during your journey of rebuilding. I love what Proverbs tells us about this in Proverbs 11:14: "Where no counsel is, the people fall: but in the multitude of counsellors there is safety." Professional guidance can provide the support and wisdom needed for effective rebuilding when needed. Therapy is not as big of a stigma as it used to be, so taking this step can provide a ton of clarity into the areas of our structure we need to potentially address.

By implementing these practical strategies, you can gain greater clarity and insight into the pieces of your current structure that may need rebuilding. Remember that the journey toward transformation is a gradual process, and each step you take brings you closer to living a more authentic and purposeful life.

Clearing Out

Before we can lay the groundwork for a new structure, we must first clear away the debris of the past. Now that we have identified the parts of our structure we need to rebuild, just as a builder removes rubble from a construction site, we must rid ourselves of the old habits, thoughts, associations, and words that no longer serve us.

In Psalm 51:10 (KJV), David writes, "Create in me a clean heart, O God; and renew a right spirit within me." This verse reminds us of the importance of purifying our hearts and minds to make room for God's transformative work.

Once we have identified what needs to be cleared out, we can begin the process of letting them go. This may involve forgiveness, both of ourselves and others, for past mistakes or wrongdoings. Ephesians 4:31–32 reminds us to "Get rid of all bitterness, rage, anger, harsh words, and slander, as well as all types of evil behavior. Instead, be kind to each other, tenderhearted, forgiving one another, just as God through Christ has forgiven you."

Clearing out the old may also mean setting boundaries and saying no to things that drain our energy or detract from our well-being. It means prioritizing self-care and making space for activities and relationships that nourish our souls. Here are some practical places to start:

> Clearing out the old may also mean setting boundaries and saying no to things that drain our energy or detract from our well-being.

1. Track your behavior: Keep a journal or use a habit-tracking app to monitor your behavior. Record instances when you engage in habits or actions that you want to change. This awareness will help you understand your triggers and the circumstances that lead to these behaviors.
2. Seek accountability: Share your desire to change with a trusted friend, family member, or mentor. Ask them to hold you accountable and provide support as you work to break old habits. Regular check-ins can help keep you motivated and accountable.
3. Replace negative habits with positive ones: Identify healthier alternatives to replace old habits. For example, if you want to reduce screen time, replace it with activities like reading, exercising, or spending time outdoors. Focus on building positive habits that align with your values and goals. Replacing bad habits with good ones will work much better than simply trying to stop.

4. Set clear goals: Establish specific, measurable goals for changing your habits. Break down larger goals into smaller, manageable steps that you can work on consistently. Celebrate your progress along the way and adjust your goals as needed.

> Replacing bad habits with good ones will work much better than simply trying to stop.

5. Create a supportive environment: Surround yourself with people and environments that support your efforts to change. Minimize exposure to situations or triggers that may tempt you to revert to old habits. Instead, seek out supportive communities and environments that encourage personal growth and positive change.
6. Practice self-compassion: Be patient and compassionate with yourself as you work to break old habits. Change takes time and effort, and setbacks are a natural part of the process. Practice self-care and self-compassion, and remember to celebrate your successes, no matter how small.

By clearing out old habits and behaviors that no longer serve you, you'll create space for new growth and transformation in your life. While exciting, this comes with a caution: some people won't understand the demolition.

CHAPTER 4

Demolition Expectations

What to Expect While in the Process

Craig Groeschel, best-selling author and pastor of LifeChurch, was once known as a partier. I mean, at his college, if you had a party, Craig was most likely involved in some way. He was known for it. He had a reputation for it.

But in his book *Divine Direction*, he tells us about when God asked him to start a Bible study in his frat house. Now, this was not only out of character but very off-brand in the eyes of his buddies.

You can imagine what his friends were thinking as he began to take steps of faith to rebuild himself according to how God was calling him. He was leading a Bible study, wearing shirts with Jesus' name on them, and becoming a bit of a "Jesus freak" in the eyes of his friends. And he was doing it…in a frat house.

Why would he do this? He was a popular guy. A leader. An athlete. A trendsetter amongst his peer group. Someone who was "on the way up" in the eyes of others. Why would he completely rebuild his life when he knew what ridicule he would face from others around him?

The answer: he knew he was called to something greater. He knew he had to choose to rebuild his life with the foundation of Jesus and that others who weren't doing the same wouldn't understand him in the process... and weren't supposed to.

Thank God he chose to tear down and rebuild because millions of people have been impacted by him and his ministry, and it all started with his obedience to tear down his structure in college and rebuild, one decision at a time.

What I found over my journey is I have not understood a lot of the things that a lot of the people around me are doing. When I was in college and had friends who chose not to go to college, I didn't understand. I graduated from high school in 2005, and back then, college was seemingly the only path to success. Or so I thought. I had a friend who decided he would go into real estate because that's what his parents did. I had friends who decided they were going to get into a trade to be an electrician or plumber because that was their passion. I had friends who decided they were just going to work at the local golf course, and that was going to be their route. I was convinced that that was not the right path.

Well, seventeen years later, my best friend, who does not have a college degree and went into real estate, owns his family's real estate business with his three brothers. One of my friends who went on to be in the trades now owns his own electrical company with forty employees.

See, I didn't understand their path because it wasn't my path. I wasn't supposed to understand it. Luckily for them, they didn't ask my permission. They didn't ask for my sponsorship.

The key point is this: If people are not on your journey, do not expect them to understand all the decisions you're making. If people are not on your journey, do not expect them to understand the changes you're making. They're not supposed to understand. God didn't give them the same assignment.

This is crucial, and it bears repeating. If you're seeking understanding from individuals who habitually mend, who strive to rectify every issue, and who resort to applying quick fixes, it often results in abandoning the path that God

> They're not supposed to understand. God didn't give them the same assignment.

has set for you. If you're trying to be understood by those people, or accepted by those people, or trying to get validation from those people, you will find yourself in a regretful pattern.

The pattern we often see is:

1. I want to do something great for God.
2. God shows me what to do in a certain area.
3. I dip my toe in the water.
4. People around me criticize me because they aren't on the same path.
5. I revert to my old ways to be accepted.
6. I lie in bed at night wondering, *What if...*

Sound familiar? If so, I get it. That is what my life looked like for many years, and sadly, it is what most people's story looks like for a lifetime.

Les Brown said it this way: "The wealthiest place on the planet is the graveyard because, in the graveyard, we will find inventions that we were never exposed to, ideas and dreams that never became a reality, and hopes and aspirations that were never acted upon."

Sad, but true.

If "fixers" are questioning your demolition to set up for your rebuild, it probably means you're on the right path. It means you're on the right path because you don't want to be on their path.

First Peter 4:4 says it this way: "Of course your former friends are surprised when you no longer plunge into the flood of wild and destructive things they do. So they slander you."

When I read this, I may tend to think, *Yeah, but I'm not stopping something destructive or wild. I haven't been wild or destructive since college (okay, maybe a little post-college, too).*

> "The wealthiest place on earth is the graveyard because, in the graveyard, we will find inventions that we were never exposed to, ideas and dreams that never became a reality, and hopes and aspirations that were never acted upon."
> Les Brown

But let's redefine those words: wild and destructive.

One of the definitions of "wild" is off an intended or expected course. So, am I living "wild" if I am floating through life without going toward God's intended direction? Am I doing "wild things" if I am, intentionally or unintentionally, living without any consistent direction going toward my purpose, and instead veering off course based on what life throws at me that day?

One of the definitions of "destructive" is to destroy. Destroying something doesn't always happen in the form of a sudden event. In fact, in our lives, destruction often comes through the compound effect of little decisions or actions that are multiplied over a long period.

> Destruction often comes through the compound effect of little decisions or actions that are multiplied over a long period.

The Bible tells us that it's the little foxes that spoil the vine (Song of Solomon 2:15).

In John 10:10, Jesus tells us that the enemy comes to "steal and kill and destroy. My purpose is to give them a rich and satisfying life."

I don't know about you, but when I define these words this way, it lines up with how I often find myself living: wildly random and destructively unintentional.

What to Expect from the Demolition

I have had a very blessed career thus far in my life. I have worked for a great company for over ten years, and within that time, I have held four different positions in four different markets. Each opportunity that I evolved into has allowed me to grow within the company and to grow as a leader.

However, there was also one other component that was consistent with all of my roles: When I told my boss

I wanted to grow and explore other opportunities to do so, their initial reaction was not great.

It wasn't because they didn't see me as being qualified or that they didn't respect my decision, but because if I left, they would have to find my replacement. And that isn't always easy.

See, we often have a part you play in people's lives whether you know it or not. Our role is normally based on our actions and habits. Our current structure is a part of their life. Our habits and actions, as they are currently constructed, serve a purpose to people.

So if we begin to change course in our habits or actions, even if it means we're bettering ourselves, it's going to leave a gap. Others are going to have to adjust. And, let's be honest, humans aren't very fond of change. So, knowing what to expect when you're breaking down an area of your life to rebuild it will help us be more prepared to navigate it. Here are a couple of basics to expect.

It's Going to Feel Weird

Full transparency: If you're used to just trying to fix things with a temporary solution to get by and have never torn down a part of your life, you will be completely out of your comfort zone. You're doing something you've never done before. Growth can only happen in an uncomfortable space.

Let's use a practical example. Try this with me. Clasp your hands together, intertwining your fingers. You've done this a thousand times. No big deal. Now, move your fingers over one.

Feels a little awkward, right? Why? Because you've always clasped your hands the same way your whole life. Even that one small shift feels a bit awkward. Imagine what tearing down years of habits in a certain area will feel like.

But, as Haggai tells Zerubbabel and the people of Jerusalem in Haggai 2:4 (TLB), "...take courage and work, for I am with you, says the Lord Almighty."

It's going to feel weird for a while, but knowing that the result will be lasting change in this area, we can have hope and take courage.

You'll Uncover Things You Tried to Forget

Losing memory happens with old age. We all go through it. A great comic strip below shows there can be humor with the coming of age when our memories aren't as sharp as they used to be.

REBUILD! DON'T REPAIR

People don't always lose their memory due to old age. Often, we lose it to protect ourselves from the pain of recalling what hurt us so badly in the past or things we did that hurt others that we would rather not bring back up. Just like sweeping dust under the rug, we often try to bury our past mistakes or undesirable behaviors.

So, the second thing you'll encounter when you start dismantling parts of the life you've built is the resurgence of things you swept under the rug. Remembering these actions may stir feelings of guilt, regret, or shame.

But here's the crucial part: when those emotions arise, remember that God offers grace. Turn to Him for forgiveness, accept it, and learn from those old pieces with confidence, knowing that digging up the past is necessary to pave the way for something greater you're rebuilding. We don't have to repeat the past, and facing it can both free us and help us learn from it.

However, as you confront these reminders of past decisions, it's vital to guard against spiraling back into old habits or thought patterns. Recognize that dwelling on past mistakes can hinder your progress and keep you stuck in a cycle of negativity. Instead, focus on the opportunity for growth and renewal that comes with rebuilding your foundation. Embrace the grace and forgiveness offered by God, and move forward with determination and faith in the journey ahead.

It's Going to Create a Mess That Will Need to Be Cleaned Up

Drive by any site where a building has been demolished. It's a mess. Dust everywhere. Beams, concrete, glass, and drywall from the old building are everywhere. So now, after the breakdown of the structure, all of this needs to be cleaned up.

This will be the same when we rebuild ourselves in an area. We will need to clean up the mess.

Maybe the mess is digging into a relationship that was soured based on previous conversations or actions. Maybe it's going to take going back to the person and apologizing for something you said or did. Maybe it's going back to forgive someone for something they did to you that you've been holding onto for years. They don't deserve forgiveness, but God will ask you to do it anyway. He will ask you to do it to make room for the new structure He wants to build in your life. He will ask you to do it because He did it for us first.

> He will ask you to do it because He did it for us first.

Maybe cleaning up the mess means admitting something you did in the past that nobody knows about except you and God, and God is going to ask you to clean that up before He can rebuild something new.

Maybe the cleanup will be admitting that a relationship is broken, coming humbly to the other person, and asking them if they would be willing to do the work of rebuilding with you.

Whatever the cleanup looks like, it's going to be messy. It's also going to be necessary. Imagine a building demolished, and instead of cleaning up the mess, the construction crew began pouring the concrete over the pile of rubble to build immediately. Wouldn't work out too well.

Here are a few things we can do practically:

1. Face the mess head-on: Don't shy away from the messiness of tearing down and rebuilding. Embrace the process, knowing that it's a necessary step towards growth and transformation.
2. Take inventory: Before rebuilding, take stock of the rubble in your life. Identify areas that need to be addressed, whether it's unhealthy habits, past mistakes, or negative thought patterns. David guides us to allow God to guide us in this assessment in Psalm 139:23–24 (NIV), when he says, "Search me, God, and know my heart: test me and know my anxious thoughts. See if there is any offensive way in me, and lead me in the way everlasting."
3. Break it down: Break the cleanup process into manageable tasks. Tackle one area at a time,

focusing on small victories along the way. This prevents overwhelm and keeps you motivated.

4. Seek support: Don't go it alone. Reach out to trusted friends, family members, or mentors for guidance and encouragement. Share your struggles and victories with others who can offer support and accountability. Believe it or not, in the right circles, more people are willing to help than we think if we would only ask.

5. Practice self-compassion: Be gentle with yourself as you navigate the messy cleanup. Understand that rebuilding takes time and effort, and setbacks are a natural part of the process. Practice self-compassion ando forgiveness as you work towards your goals. "The Lord is compassionate and gracious, slow to anger, abounding in love" (Psalm 103:8, NIV). Extend to yourself the same compassion and grace that God freely offers to you.

> Extend to yourself the same compassion and grace that God freely offers to you.

6. Learn from mistakes: Use the cleanup process as an opportunity for self-reflection and growth. Reflect on past mistakes and consider what les-

sons you can learn from them. Use these insights to make positive changes moving forward.

7. Stay committed: Stay committed to the cleanup process, even when it feels challenging or overwhelming. Keep your eyes on the ultimate goal of building a stronger, healthier foundation for your life. Galatians 6:9 (NIV) says it best: "Let us not become weary in doing good, for at the proper time we will reap a harvest if we do not give up."

By implementing these practical tips, you can navigate the messy cleanup process with confidence and resilience, paving the way for a brighter future ahead.

So Now You Have "Nothing"

Picture yourself standing amidst the rubble of what was once your home—a place filled with twenty years of memories. The walls have been torn down, and the debris cleared away, leaving nothing but a barren landscape. No traces of the life that once lived within these walls remain. You stand alone, surrounded by the echoes of the past, on a desolate concrete foundation that serves as a stark reminder of what once was.

So what is next?

You have two choices: build another structure on the old foundation or do the work to tear up the foundation and lay a new one.

> You have two choices: build another structure on the old foundation or do the work to tear up the foundation and lay a new one.

The decision should lie in what kind of structure you want to build now.

Do you want to build the same kind of structure as before? If so, demolishing the old one was kind of silly.

Or do you want to build a structure that can last for generations? A structure that people will be able to tell is solid. A structure your kids and grandkids can look at and say, "Grandma built that part of our legacy right!" "Grandpa was intentional with that part of our family's history. He built something of meaning and impact there."

If the new version is going to be bigger, better, and more stable than the old one, that means we have one more piece to dig up before we can begin to rebuild: we have to dig into the foundation.

CHAPTER 5

Dealing with the Old Foundation

Will It Support Your Envisioned Destiny

Dealing with old things from our past is never an easy adventure. Sometimes, it even makes you re-live a memory of shame that you had forgotten about for years. However, facing these memories and the foundations they have built is crucial to the process of re-building your life on a stronger, more faithful base.

Our past experiences, both good and bad, shape the foundations of our current lives. This foundation influences the structure of our habits, our associations, our thoughts, and our words. Ignoring these past experiences or attempting to forget them doesn't make their impact go away; it only buries them temporarily. Much like a house built on an unstable foundation, the cracks will eventually appear, and the structure will falter if these underlying issues are not addressed.

The Importance of Acknowledging the Past

The Bible frequently calls us to reflect on and learn from our past. In Isaiah 43:18–19 (NIV), we read, "Forget the former things; do not dwell on the past. See, I am doing a new thing! Now it springs up; do you not perceive it?" This passage reminds us that while we should not be consumed by our past, acknowledging it allows us to recognize and embrace the new things God is doing in our lives.

Consider the story of Joseph in Genesis. Betrayed by his brothers and sold into slavery, Joseph endured years of hardship. Yet, he did not let his painful past define him. Instead, he acknowledged it and allowed God to use it for a greater purpose. Genesis 50:20 (NIV) illustrates this beautifully: "You intended to harm me, but God intended it for good to accomplish what is now being done, the saving of many lives." Joseph's ability to face his past and understand its role in God's plan enabled him to build a stronger future.

Lesson Two from the Escalade

Remember that Cadillac truck with the crazy payment a few chapters back? Well, there is a side to the story I left out. It is the most painful part but is also the most transformative.

So, here I was, six months deep into my cycle of shame and pride, still trying to keep up appearances while drowning in financial turmoil. One night, around midnight, my friend called me from a college bar nearby, a familiar spot of ours. He needed a ride, and although I was tired, I agreed to pick him up. I drove to the bar, which was located within a strip plaza, and found a spot to park. After shooting him a quick text, I sat and waited for him to walk out.

Little did I know, my car had a feature I hadn't paid much attention to before—it automatically unlocked all four doors when parked. This was a routine I'd done countless times before, but this time, it would lead to a pivotal moment in my journey of rebuilding.

I'm sitting there, waiting in my truck, the minutes ticking by, thinking nothing of it. Suddenly, I hear it—the passenger door swings open with a creak, followed by the ominous click of the back door unlatching. My heart skips a beat as I assume it's my friend, but in a heartbeat, I realize something's wrong. Two strangers emerge, their faces obscured by masks, their hands gripping guns with intensity in their eyes. Time seems to slow to a crawl as they cock their weapons and level them at my head with chilling precision.

Fear grips me as I realize this isn't a nightmare—it's a nightmare come to life. My senses heighten, every sound, every movement amplified in the deafening silence of the moment. I'm frozen in terror, my mind reeling as the harsh reality sinks in.

We drive to the ATM, their demands ringing in my ears. With trembling hands, I withdraw the maximum amount, my heart pounding in my chest like a drumbeat of dread. They command me to drive to the end of a desolate service road, and with each passing moment, my pulse quickens with the sickening certainty of my impending fate.

As we reach the dead end, I step out of the truck, my legs like jelly beneath me. Guns trained on me from both sides, I surrender everything—my keys, my phone, my wallet, my dignity. My body trembles uncontrollably as I press my hands against the cold metal of the truck, the weight of their threats suffocating me with each passing second.

Time stretches on, an agonizing eternity of uncertainty and fear. Every minute feels like an hour, every second an eternity of dread. I'm on the brink of collapse, teetering on the edge of oblivion as I await my fate.

Finally, the moment passes, the tension dissipates slowly. With trembling limbs, I turn to find nothing but empty darkness behind me. Relief floods through me like a tidal wave as I stumble back towards the bar, my senses still on high alert, every shadow a potential threat.

And then, a glimmer of hope—a beacon of light in the darkness. My keys, my phone, my wallet—all discarded in a bush like discarded remnants of a nightmare. I snatch them up with trembling hands, my pulse still racing with the aftershocks of terror.

With shaky breaths, I return to my truck, every nerve on edge, every instinct screaming for me to flee. But I press on, driving back to the safety of the bar, the flashing lights of a police car offering a sliver of solace in the night.

As I recount the harrowing ordeal to the officers, my friend appears, his concern etched on his face. The night's events spill out in a torrent of words, each syllable a reminder of the horrors endured. The police search fruitlessly for the perpetrators, their faces lost to the shadows, their identities swallowed by the darkness.

And yet, despite the terror that still grips me, there's a glimmer of hope—a flicker of resilience in the face of adversity. Though the scars of that night may never fully heal, I cling to the hope that one day, the shadows will recede, and the light of justice will prevail.

I remember calling my father at two o'clock in the morning that day once I got home.

I told him, "Dad, I just got robbed. I don't know what happened. I'm okay, but I was petrified."

He said, as calmly as anything, "Were you in your truck?"

I said, "Yeah."

His reply was, "Of course you did."

"What? What do you mean, 'Of course I did?'" I scoffed back.

He said, "You wanted to be seen, and you were seen." I was speechless!

He went on to explain that when people saw me in that truck, and I thought they admired me, what I didn't realize is what it does is draw attention to me, and not all attention is good attention. In their eyes, they saw not just a vehicle but a symbol of materialism and ostentation. They saw a facade of wealth and status that obscured the true essence of who I was as a person. Instead of admiration, what they may have perceived was a superficiality that spoke more of insecurity than genuine confidence.

I had just experienced the bad side of attention, and I didn't like it. Sometimes, when we hang on to something so desperately that it creates an identity in us that is so far from God, He has to do some pretty drastic things to get our attention and begin to bring us back in alignment with Himself.

> It's not punishment. It's preparation.

It's not punishment. It's preparation.

Hebrews 12 talks about how God disciplines His children and that it is good for us that He does this, for He disciplines who He loves. He summarizes it beautifully in verse 11 when He says, "No discipline is enjoyable while it is happening—it's painful! But afterward there will be a quiet harvest of peaceful living for those who are trained in this way."

Within a week, I got rid of the truck. I came home and admitted to my parents what I had done. I had begged for money from my grandmother to pay off my credit cards, I couldn't pay the truck loan, and all the things I had done just to "keep up with the Joneses." I finally came to the place where my image had to be built on something different than status. It was time to begin tearing some things down and begin my rebuild.

There's a First Time for Everything

The truth is, most of us have never taken the time to research and dig deep to understand what our foundation is made of.

How could we? We have been building up the structure of our lives on it for decades. It's been buried underneath our structures built by our actions, habits, and relationships.

So, if we force ourselves to look deep within and see it for the first time, it is usually unfamiliar and often scary.

"What is this? Where did it come from? What do I do with it?" Those were the three questions I had as I began doing this work in my own life. There are a couple of thought processes and techniques I'll share with you that began to work for me as I started on this journey throughout the rest of the chapter. Let's start with figuring out how our foundations are often formed.

Your Foundation Wasn't Initially Framed by *You*

Back in chapter 3, we talked a bit about this, but it is such a critical piece that it's worth repeating and digging into: a lot of your foundation wasn't laid by *you.*

The reason this is key is that it should permit us to look squarely at it. Often, we don't want to look at things when they reveal something we did wrong or something embarrassing about ourselves. The good news is that many of the initial parts of our foundation weren't put in place by us.

We don't get to choose how we enter this world. We don't get to choose our parents or the city we lived in when we were kids. We don't get to choose the schools we went to or the neighborhood we grew up in. We don't get to choose how our parents raised us. All those are uncontrollable factors.

While some of our foundations may not be our fault, it is our responsibility. It's our responsibility to evaluate, address it, and change it, if needed, based on the life we want to live.

Although all those pieces are often out of our control, along the way, we also make choices. While we may have been too young, in some instances, to truly know their impact, they would either reinforce your foundation or begin to create a new one. Things like the music we listened to, the movies we watched, the books we read, and the friends we hung out with.

> While some of our foundations may not be our fault, it is our responsibility.

All of these things are what shaped the foundation of our current selves. Let's be honest, some of us have a more solid foundation than others, whether by decisions or circumstances. So, some will have more foundation to dig up than others. Either way, God will honor the work we do, as He knows where you're starting from. And He has been gracious enough to give us some practical ways of doing the work. We will dig into these next.

Reverse Engineering Behavior

When I first started going to therapy in my thirties for this work of rebuilding myself, I wanted to know why I was doing some of the things I was doing.

I was in a church service, and the message referenced Romans 12:2, "Don't copy the behavior and customs of this world, but let God transform you into a new person by changing the way you think. Then you will learn to know God's will for you, which is good and pleasing and perfect."

While that verse was so powerful, I didn't know how to do that. I needed to go somewhere to get the tools to allow myself to change my thinking. I needed help.

I felt like Paul when he wrote in Romans 7:15, "I don't really understand myself, for I want to do what is right, but I don't do it. Instead, I do what I hate." Do you ever feel like that?

I couldn't have identified with that sentiment more. Maybe that's where you are today, too.

So I wanted to know why. My counselor began the work of understanding me and what I was going through, and then he gave me a lens I had never seen through before. He taught me why I was doing what I was doing. He taught me how to actually examine each behavior intentionally to get to the root of why I was doing it. And it was *all* biblical.

The part of this passage he helped reveal to me was the whole *transformation* thing. I began to get new tools in my toolbelt to do it.

He introduced me to the basics of cognitive behavioral therapy.

Cognitive behavioral therapy (CBT) is a widely used and evidence-based form of psychotherapy that focuses on the connection between thoughts, feelings, and behaviors. It is grounded in the idea that our thoughts influence our emotions and behaviors, and by changing negative thought patterns, we can alleviate emotional distress and improve overall well-being.

How to Transform

The behaviors we have are a result of a feeling we have rooted in a thought that came from a certain event (see diagram 5.1). The event can be big or small, unusual or typical. And most of the time, we can't control what events happen around us. We can't control if we hit traffic on the way home from work. We can't control how our child behaves. We can't control if we wake up sick or a little under the weather. We can't control *most* things in our day to day.

We also can't control the feeling that is attached to a thought. If I think something is a huge deal that is going to be a big disappointment in my life, a sad or depressed feeling is usually going to accompany that thought. Your brain believes what you feed it.

So, while we can't control the events in our lives and can't control the feelings that come with the thoughts we have, we *can* control the thoughts we have about what happens to us and can, therefore, control the responding action that flows through it.

Cognitive Behavior Cycle (5.1)

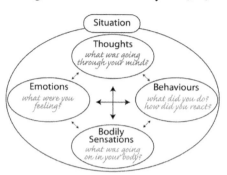

Let's use an example: if someone cuts you off in traffic tomorrow morning, you have a choice of how to think about that.

Option 1: *That guy is a selfish idiot who doesn't care about anyone else and keeping people safe. I hope he gets pulled over!*

Option 2: *If someone is willing to do something so crazy, he must have an emergency he is trying to get to. I hope he gets there soon and everything is okay.*

Let's see how both of those responses may play out.

Option 1

Event: You get cut off in traffic on your way to work.

Thought: *That guy is a selfish idiot who doesn't care about anyone else and keeping people safe. I hope he gets pulled over!*

Feeling: You're angry, frustrated, and annoyed.

Response: The next interaction you have that morning is going to have some annoyance and frustration. Heck, maybe that lasts all morning or, for some, even all day.

Option 2

Event: You get cut off in traffic on your way to work.

Thought: *If someone is willing to do something so crazy, he must have an emergency he is trying to get to. I hope he gets there soon and everything is okay.*

Feeling: concern for someone else and their well-being.

Response: The next interaction you have will carry with it that feeling of concern for others.

See the difference? In that one little example, with the same event, intentionally choosing to think differently about it makes a world of difference in the downstream effects that part of your day has on the rest of your day.

Slow Down to Speed Up

At the heart of our transformation lies intentionality—a deliberate choice to reshape the very pathways of our minds. Consider our brains as intricate maps, etched over time by repeated thoughts and actions. These

> At the heart of transformation lies intentionality-a deliberate choice to reshape the very pathways of our minds.

pathways, like worn-out paths in a field, become deeply ingrained, guiding our responses almost instinctively. Yet, if we aspire to align ourselves with God's purpose, we must embark on a new journey, carving out fresh pathways through intentional thought and action. It's similar to forging a new trail in familiar terrain; it's challenging yet essential for growth.

In the realm of addiction recovery, this process is magnified due to the intensity of the need of the patient to shift their behavior. Rehab programs spanning ninety days recognize the brain's need for this duration to reconstruct itself. Through intentional effort, individuals learn to navigate life's challenges with newfound resilience and positivity, gradually replacing old patterns with healthier ones. This principle extends beyond addiction, influencing every habit we form—each demanding our conscious intention to reshape our mental landscape.

Let's look at the two things God asks His people to look at when considering whether or not they need to rebuild His temple.

1. Consider How Things Are Going for You

We were about one year into living in our first home and had been having trouble growing our grass after the first winter. I just assumed that it was because of the cold weather and the new sod not getting enough water. I increased my watering time over the subsequent weeks only to find that there was no better result than before. And now my water bill was higher, too.

Doing my research, I read that at times the dirt can be too compressed for the water to get underneath the top layer of the soil to get down where the roots can grow, which can stunt the growth of the grass. Not knowing anything about it, my first step was to go buy a rake with thick barbs on it to put in the ground to try to alleviate some of the pressure of the soil. As I was doing so (looking dumb to the neighbors the whole way through), I hit something hard in my grass. Not hard like it was hard to push through the soil. Hard like a solid mass. I moved forward another three or four inches and went down again with the rake, only to hit the same hard-feeling item. Three inches forward from there, the same result.

Something was under there. Was it a rock? Something else? Who knew? Honestly, the little boy inside me hoped that it was a treasure chest like I had seen in all the cartoons and the kids' shows that I had watched as a kid.

Spoiler alert: It was not.

However, when I dug down deeper, I found a solid piece of wood. It was a log about two and a half feet long and between eight and ten inches in diameter. I could tell very easily that the builders had just thrown the log into the yard, and instead of taking it out before they laid the sod on top, they just thought the sod would grow over it and that nobody would know the difference. Needless to say, after I took the log out of my yard, I had a gaping hole in my yard for a little while that I had to fill in with new soil.

If the exterior results of what we're seeing, experiencing, feeling, and harvesting are not what we think they should be based on what we're doing, it probably means something underneath the surface that must be dealt with. The lack of grass growth on my lawn had less to do with the grass and more to do with what was beneath the surface. Is the soil too compressed? Are there enough nutrients in the soil? Am I watering enough or too much? Or is there a huge log that needs to be dealt with?

So many times, we try to treat what's on the surface of our lives and fix something that is a byproduct of something else. We don't take the time needed to think about what is under the surface, causing the problem.

We mentioned this in the last chapter, but it bears repeating. In the book of Haggai, God speaks through the prophet Haggai and very plainly tells the Israelite people to inspect this very same thing as He begins His message to them about rebuilding His temple. Haggai 1:5 says it this way: "This is what the Lord of Heaven's Armies says: Look at what's happening to you!"

It is His divine direction to inspect our fruit, and if something is off, maybe it's time to consider rebuilding His temple (that's us) all the way down to the foundation.

2. Consider How Your Actions Align with God's Word

This seems simple, but it can often be the missing ingredient to knowing the next move. We sometimes run to others for advice, which is great, especially if they're trustworthy. But let's not skip the step of going to God and His Word first.

Before we go to the phone, let's first go to the throne.

Here are a couple of examples.

If I'm constantly getting angry at my children for the things they're doing, flying off the handle, and responding in unhealthy ways, then trying to fix my anger will be a temporary solution at best and a failed attempt at worst. What I need to do is figure out why my instant reaction is anger. I need to get down below the surface of my action to the foundation of why this is happening. If I know anger isn't how God's Word instructed me to parent (see Ephesians 6:4) and I know that I have peace inside me (through the Holy Spirit),

> Before we go to the phone, let's first go to the throne.

then something is creating this automatic response. It's my job to dig deep enough to find it and rebuild.

Was there something traumatic in my life at a younger age that taught me to react this way when things annoy me? When facing frustration, was there an example set by someone at home, school, or from a friend that said successful people act this way?

Let's apply this same introspection to something like our relationship with money and possessions. Are we acting as though the money we earn is solely ours, or do we recognize it as a gift from God? Are we operating from a mindset of abundance or scarcity?

Consider this: If you're anything like me, you may find that your natural inclination is to feel more secure when you have more money. Having savings or a robust retirement fund can provide a sense of safety. While being financially prepared for the future is prudent, there's a danger in placing too much trust in our financial resources rather than in our Creator.

For instance, let's say you grew up in a household where money was a constant source of tension and fear. Perhaps your parents struggled to make ends meet, and you witnessed their anxiety over finances. As a result, you develop a subconscious belief that accumulating wealth is the key to security and happiness. This belief may manifest in behaviors such as hoarding money or prioritizing financial success above all else.

Similarly, our children observe our attitudes and behaviors towards money. If they see us placing excessive importance on material possessions or constantly striving for more wealth, they may internalize these values and adopt similar habits. Thus, we need to model healthy attitudes towards money and possessions rooted in gratitude, stewardship, and trust in God's provision.

Just as we must examine the root causes of our anger to become better parents, we must also confront the underlying beliefs and attitudes driving our financial decisions and anything else that is making our foundation what it is today. By digging deep and rebuilding our mindset around these things, we can cultivate a healthier relationship with them and model godly stewardship for future generations.

One Week Challenge

With intentionality in mind, I'd like to offer you to take part in a One Week Challenge to begin rebuilding our foundations, while reshaping our thoughts. Here is what it looks like.

Action Steps:

1. Prepare your workspace: Sit down with a blank sheet of paper or use a copy of the worksheet on page 69.

2. Identify regular events:
   - At the top of the page, write down the facts of a situation that recently happened or that happens regularly.
3. Record what your original thought is:
   - In the left column, in the top box, write down your initial thoughts.
4. Identify associated feelings:
   - In the left "Feeling" box, list the emotions linked to your current responses.
5. Examine your associated behavior:
   - In the left "Behavior" column, write down your typical or initial response to these events.
6. Generate alternative thoughts:
   - To the right of the initial thought, brainstorm alternative perspectives that could lead to more positive outcomes.
7. Explore associated feelings:
   - In the right "Feeling" box, consider how these new thoughts would make you feel.
8. Envision alternative responses:
   - In the right "Response" column, visualize how your reactions would differ based on these new thoughts and feelings.

I have included an example of my worksheet here for reference. What a difference changing our thoughts makes, even when the same events come up in our lives!

The Cognitive Model
Worksheet

Name _____   Date _____

SITUATION
Something happen. This step covers only the facts of what happened, without any interpretation.

↓ ↓

THOUGHT
Using thought, you interpret the situation. These interpretation are not always accurate. There are many ways to think about the same situation.

| MY ACTUAL THOUGHT | ALTERNATE THOUGHT |

↓ ↓

FEELING
You experience emotions based upon your thoughts about the situation.

↓ ↓

BEHAVIOR
You respond to the situation based upon your thoughts and feelings.

The Work Will Be Worth It

So, if you went through that exercise with me, you may be wondering how the heck you're supposed to do this in everyday life. Unless we're going to have dozens of printed worksheets around us at all times, how are we supposed to apply this in real, everyday life?

Well, it's going to take practice. And a lot of it. I would encourage you to take ten minutes at the beginning of each day and go through this exercise for something that you know could trigger a negative response if it doesn't go just right. Decide, *ahead of time*, that your thought will be one of the alternatives and the one on autopilot.

Then, at the end of the day, take ten minutes to evaluate your day. How did you respond? Was it what you wanted it to be, or not quite? If not, what feeling led to it, and what thought triggered that feeling? And next time that happens, what could an alternate thought be that could lead down a better path?

Also, remember, your current foundation took years of consistent brain paths being built, so as we are dealing with that old foundation and working to rebuild a new one, give yourself some grace. We don't have to be perfect every day. The important thing is to be consistent. If we walk our new path each day by changing the way we think, we will begin to see our old founda-

> We don't have to be perfect every day. The important thing is to be consistent.

tion fade away and our new foundation lead us in the direction of our purpose.

As we reflect on the foundations and structures that have guided us thus far, it's essential to acknowledge their role in our lives. While they may have served us well in previous seasons, we must recognize that our aspirations, dreams, and God's calling may demand a different foundation—one built on faith, resilience, and authenticity. Embracing the necessity of rebuilding allows us to step boldly into the future, prepared to embrace the blessings and challenges that lie ahead with a sturdy and purposeful foundation beneath us.

CHAPTER 6

The Lonely Work: Where Most People Run Back

In the story of Moses parting the Red Sea, if you slow down enough to picture the scene, you may find something interesting. While it was an unbelievably miraculous thing God did to deliver the Israelites from the situation by parting the Red Sea, the people still had to walk through. He didn't make them do it. They stood before a God-created path, with walls of water on both sides, dry ground below their feet, and a path that was so long they couldn't see to the other side. They saw the miraculous opportunity and had a choice: do we enter into the Red Sea between the walls of water, having faith that God will keep these walls up all night while we walk across, not being able to see where the end was, or do we go back to slavery?

On the surface, it may seem obvious, but they had already been complaining to Moses for taking them out of Egypt. While the bondage of slavery was brutal, the familiarity of routine was often tempting when the unknown was the alternative.

And when they chose, there was a point in the walk where they were so far from the side of the Red Sea that they left that they began not to be able to see it. Furthermore, the Red Sea was so wide that they were still miles from the other side, so they also couldn't see how far they had to go or what was on the other side.

They were at a decision point. And at this point in our rebuilding, we will have to make a similar decision. We are far enough down the path that we are beginning to see our past selves disappear, but we don't know how far away the finish line is or what lies on the other side.

Do we continue the journey or go back to the familiar?

This is an important point in our journey, as acknowledging the fact that there is a lonely season here, I believe, is crucial. Being lonely is not fun, especially if

> Will you continue the journey or go back to the familiar?

we have been accepted by people we liked in the past. Those people whom we have spent a lot of time with are now questioning our choices. They may be gossiping about you to others in your group. They may be trying to convince you not to change. They may even be accusing you of thinking you're better than other people.

Let me encourage you: If that is what you experience as you begin to rebuild, you're on the right path. Jesus is specific in telling us that the road that leads to life is narrow.

Robert Frost said it beautifully in his iconic poem *The Road Not Taken*.

> Two roads diverged in a yellow wood,
> And sorry I could not travel both
> And be one traveler, long I stood
> And looked down one as far as I could
> To where it bent in the undergrowth;
>
> Then took the other, as just as fair,
> And having perhaps the better claim,
> Because it was grassy and wanted wear;
> Though as for that the passing there
> Had worn them really about the same,
>
> And both that morning equally lay
> In leaves no step had trodden black.
> Oh, I kept the first for another day!
> Yet knowing how way leads on to way,
> I doubted if I should ever come back.
>
> I shall be telling this with a sigh

Somewhere ages and ages hence:
Two roads diverged in a wood, and I—
I took the one less traveled by,
And that has made all the difference.

In Haggai, when the people were rebuilding the Lord's temple, it appears that the Lord knew that they were going to need His comfort in the middle of the rebuilding process. He steps in about a month after they start and tells them to take courage. The reason He does that, I believe, in such a short amount of time is based on human nature.

Isn't it amazing how quickly people can turn on you when you're not aligning with what they want to do or how they want to live? While people may criticize and ridicule you for maybe a week or two, after a little while, they often just discard you. This can hurt worse than the ridicule at times. So now you're out in the wilderness trying to do the right thing, and your friends, colleagues, and sometimes, even loved ones are distancing themselves from you.

You may feel more lonely than ever.

In those moments, I think we have to find comfort in the one that created us and in the one that we're trying to please as we're rebuilding ourselves instead of repairing. If we go to Him to seek comfort, He will give it to us, just like He did with His people. Here are some practical ways we can do that:

1. Seek solace in prayer: Set aside time each day to pray and connect with God. Pour out your heart to Him, sharing your struggles, fears, and uncertainties. Trust that He is always listening and ready to provide comfort and guidance.
2. Reflect on Scripture: Spend time reading and meditating on passages from the Bible that offer words of comfort and encouragement. Allow God's promises to fill you with hope and reassurance during difficult times. The Psalms are a great place to find some comfort. Reading some of those gives me comfort, knowing David was definitely in a lonely place at times, but his faith in God is what helped him get through.
3. Practice gratitude: Cultivate a spirit of gratitude by intentionally focusing on the blessings in your life, even amidst challenges. Keep a gratitude journal or make it a habit to verbally express thanks to God for His provision and presence.
4. Lean on community: Surround yourself with supportive friends, family members, or fellow believers who can offer love, encouragement, and prayer support during times of rebuilding. Don't hesitate to reach out for help when needed, even if it's a little uncomfortable.
5. Find comfort in worship: Allow music, hymns, or worship songs to minister to your soul and

uplift your spirit. Spend time in worship, singing praises to God and allowing His presence to bring comfort and healing to your heart. Music can be a powerful thing to lift your spirit.
6. Trust in God's promises: Remind yourself of God's faithfulness and promises as you journey through the rebuilding process. Trust that He is with you every step of the way, guiding and sustaining you with His love and grace.

By implementing these practical application ideas, we can find comfort and strength in God's presence as we rebuild where we need to, trusting in His faithfulness and provision.

The other amazing thing is that while He will give us comfort, He will also test us in those seasons. It's easy to go back to old habits and behaviors because that is where you were comfortable. Those things bring familiarity but do not necessarily lead you to your purpose, as it is not your destiny. So, while it is comfortable to be the person you used to be because the friends, situations, and circumstances are comfortable, it is also something that

> Along this road of moving toward your destiny, it is just that: *your* destiny.

is diabolically opposed to what you know you were created to do.

To move forward to the next step, we must acknowledge that loneliness is real, and we must be prepared to move forward despite our desires to be comfortable so as to truly push for the life God has prepared for us.

You're Not *Really* Alone

When I was early in this journey, I was hungry for God's purpose in my life (full disclosure: I am still early in this journey). So, there was a time, after I had gotten involved in the church, where I got what I believed was a revelation from God, proceeded by a series of events that taught me so much that I wanted to share it.

I had just begun a friendship with my lead pastor at the time, and I wanted to share these things with him. I thought an easy way was by inviting him to lunch and sharing what God had shown me.

It wasn't abnormal for him to have lunch with people, so I was sure this was a no-brainer.

That Sunday, I asked if he had time for lunch, and he explained that he had a staff meeting on Tuesday, building meetings on Wednesday, and a service run-through on Thursday, so that week, he couldn't do lunch.

I was devastated!

I mean, the Lord had given me this experience, and sharing it with my lead pastor made sense…at least to me.

So I drove out of the parking lot, admittedly defeated.

As I was driving on the main road, the Holy Spirit spoke to my spirit and said, "Um. You know, I am free for lunch on Wednesday."

What?!

The Holy Spirit proceeded to show me the real reason He shut the door of having lunch with my pastor: pride.

He began to show me that, along this road of moving toward my destiny, it was just that: *my* destiny. While it was exciting to me, I also had to realize that others had their destinies to chase after as well.

While I was chasing my purpose, the only person God wanted me fully reliant on for support, encouragement, and counsel was Him.

Find Your New Community

Imagine, for a moment, being Mary, like Jesus' mother, Mary. While exciting and scary, how lonely it must have felt after Michael the angel revealed to her what would shortly happen. Who would understand? She would surely feel like she couldn't tell anyone. Would she disgrace Joseph?

Then, this miracle gift from God begins to change her. Like physically. She begins to crave things she hadn't before. She begins to look different. Her moods change. Her sleep changes. And soon, she began to struggle to hide her baby bump.

See, when we go through a rebuilding, it is often due to something choosing us. It is because God has put something inside us that is becoming so tough to conceal that we need to rebuild part of our lives to support it so we can properly birth it. If we don't rebuild what we need to and choose not to birth it, that destiny inside us will die, and we will always wonder.

Luke shows us an important backstory in his depiction by first letting us know about the story of John the Baptist's birth.

Luke chapter 1 outlines for us that Elizabeth, Mary's relative, became pregnant after going through the change of life. This was a miracle after being barren for all her life, as she was now well advanced in age. This is important because it shows us that, while it may not seem like it, there are people who are also going through similar rebuilding processes. For me, it gives me hope.

> There is nothing worse than trying to rebuild your life to align with God's direction and only being around stagnant people.

Luke explains that when Mary heard that Elizabeth was pregnant, she hurried to meet Elizabeth.

Big lesson here: if we find out someone is going through something or headed in a direction similar to ours, we would be wise to prioritize associating with those people. There is nothing worse than trying to rebuild your life to align with God's direction and only being around stagnant people.

Luke's account shows us in Luke 1:41 that "At the sound of Mary's greeting, Elizabeth's child leaped within her, and Elizabeth was filled with the Holy Spirit."

When we get around people who are going through similar journeys as we are, it often ignites something in us that we couldn't have otherwise gotten. We need people with us, especially when we are rebuilding something in our lives. But who these people are that are around us plays a critical role. If we have done the work to break down our old structure and deal with our old foundation, now is not the time to just be around whoever is willing to hang out. We better ensure that we are intentional about getting around people who know what we're going through, and while they can empathize with the tough stuff, they can also encourage us to continue the journey and have strength along the way.

There's a life on the other side of this rebuild that you cannot have if you're not willing to go through this season. There is a promise on the other side of this that is so far above what you used to have in your previous life that you can't comprehend it. The problem is that even if you know and have faith that it will be there, it's still a difficult season to navigate day after day. When we remember we serve an all-knowing God who sees our heart, it makes it a little easier to navigate this season. Be encouraged that this season will serve as a piece toward the future God holds for us and will work together with other pieces to complete His perfect plan.

So, what do you do to stay encouraged? Three things can help us get through this lonely phase as we're navigating the season towards the rebuilding of the person that we are.

1. Continue to Pray

In any season that we're lonely, I believe God wants us to express to Him all of our feelings, whether good or bad. God knows when we're frustrated. God knows when we're angry. God knows when we're sad. God knows when we're lonely. God knows when you're happy. God knows when you're content. God knows when you're frustrated. God knows when you're greedy. God knows when you are perverted. God knows when you are joyous. God knows when you're forgiving, and God knows when we hold grudges.

God knows what we're going through, and He understands because Jesus went through it just like we do.

To not talk to the Creator of the universe honestly about what we're going through is a huge mistake, especially when there may be limited people that we can talk to during the season. He wants you to express what you're feeling. You're not surprising God by telling Him you're sad. He knows you're sad. You're not surprising God when you tell Him you're frustrated and angry and don't understand what He's bringing you through.

Don't believe me? Glance at the Psalms. David was very honest with God at the beginning of many of his Psalms about how angry, frustrated, and sad he was. As he was talking to the Lord, it became very apparent that honest communication helped David come out of that mental and emotional state into one of worship, praise, and trust.

> You're not surprising God by telling Him you're sad.

Notice that David often didn't start with praise. His honesty led him there. He laid his emotion at the feet of the Lord, and with that release, he was able to praise and trust Him through often unbearable worldly circumstances.

> David often didn't start with praise. His honesty led him there.

The first thing we need to do when we are leaving some people behind while we rebuild is to continue to pray.

2. Remind Yourself of the Desired Destination

In our foundational story, God reminds the people in Jerusalem about what the end goal looks like in Haggai 2:9, where it says, "The future glory of this Temple will be greater than its past glory, says the Lord of Heaven's Armies. And in this place I will bring peace. I, the Lord of Heaven's Armies, have spoken!" God wants us to keep our focus on the end goal, especially when it starts to feel lonely.

We read as Jesus is talking to God in the Garden of Gethsemane, He asks God to take the cup from Him. He doesn't want to go to the cross. His earthly flesh knows the pain, suffering, and embarrassment He would endure, and yet, in His ultimate example, He says, "Yet I want your will to be done, not mine" (Luke 22:42).

It's so important that we understand that keeping our eyes on the destination and putting one foot in front of the other is sometimes the only thing that keeps us going. It's hard to imagine the destination some days. And those are the days when we have to dig in and take some time to ourselves to refocus our thoughts and words toward the person we are rebuilding ourselves to be.

3. Take It One Day at a Time

David Goggins is an ultra-marathon runner, which means his marathons are between 100 and 150 miles per race. These races can often take well over a day in time, and he has been world-renowned for pushing his body to the limit through these races. He was asked in an interview at one point, what kept him going, and his answer was profound.

David said at some point all he focuses on is putting one foot in front of the other. He can't focus on the race. He can't focus on the distance left. He can't focus on the pain he's going through, the cold, the darkness, the dehydration, or any other physical circumstance. The only thing he can focus on is putting one foot in front of the other.

That's what we will need to do in this season. There will be times when all we need to do is focus on one foot in front of the other. I don't know if I can make it the rest of the day, but I know I can do this for the next hour. I don't know if I can make it the rest of the way, but I know I can do this today. I don't know how long it's going to be. I'm going to focus on doing what God's asking me to do to rebuild today, this hour, this minute.

See, I don't know how long this rebuild is going to take. That is the hardest part of the rebuild. If God gave us a timeline and said this is going to take six months or a year or two years, we may be able to calculate it and calibrate it in our minds and prepare, but that wouldn't take faith. It takes faith to operate day to day during the rebuild, knowing that God has a plan for us. God has a plan for this rebuilding, and He's going to honor our effort and our intention as we rebuild, and we have to leave that in His hands. Taking it day by day helps us not to lose hope. It allows us to feel like we are taking one step every day toward the desired outcome that God has, knowing that that desired outcome that God has is so far beyond what our imagination can fathom.

Let me encourage you as we wrap up the tips to navigate the lonely season. Everyone goes through it, whether you're rebuilding or not. Everyone will go through a season or two or three that will be lonely. This book is all about what is on the other side when we go through it and how to finish the work.

The other kind of loneliness will happen when you know you're destined for more but are unwilling to go through the rebuilding process. That loneliness will happen every single night that you lie on your bed. Just you with your thoughts, your emotions, your regrets. That regret cycle we talked about in chapter 4 will create a loneliness that nobody wants.

They say the number one regret in life for older people as they're nearing the end of their journey here on Earth is that they didn't take risks. That they didn't do things that they thought they wanted to do because of fear. Fear of other people's judgment. Fear of failure. Fear of exposure.

We have to make a decision. Let me rephrase: We get to make a decision. There will be loneliness in our lives at some point. We might as well go through it on our way to fulfilling our purpose.

This is where it starts to get fun. Not because it is necessarily easier but because we are beginning to reshape how we're wired and are getting our energy from walking toward being who we were created to be.

> There will be loneliness in our lives at some point. We might as well go through it on our way to fulfilling our purpose.

Jesus illustrates it beautifully in John's account of the woman at the well. Jesus stopped at Jacob's well, in Samaria, on His way to Galilee. He was tired from His journey, and He stopped to get water. As He encounters the Samaritan woman and reveals Himself to be the Messiah, His disciples urge Him to eat, to give Him strength and nourishment.

His response was one we can all learn from: "My nourishment comes from doing the will of God, who sent me, and from finishing his work" (John 4:34).

See, when we do what God asks us to, the amount of energy given to us is amazing! As we go through this journey, let's continue to remind ourselves that this rebuilding in one or many parts of our lives is so we can live out our purpose. It's a purpose given to us by the Creator. So, while the work can be arduous at times, our strength comes from doing the work to build the foundation on which His temple can stand tall.

Building Up

CHAPTER 7

A New Foundation

Begin with the End in Mind

We have all driven by construction sites that had been cleared to build something new, and every day you drove by it, there seemed to be no progress made. The trees were cleared off the land. The dirt was smoothed over every day. You drove by, and there seemed to be the same tractors, bulldozers, and dump trucks in the same place. We often wonder, *What in the world is happening to this? Did this build get stalled for some reason? When are they going to finish finally?*

After a while, the foundation just looks like it's sitting there.

I think our understanding of what a foundation is and what it takes to build one needs to align very much with the foundational elements required in buildings.

Let's use the analogy we have prior and compare the foundations needed to build a house vs. a skyscraper.

The average depth of a foundation for a single-family home is about 12–18 inches deep. The depth of a foundation for a skyscraper goes between 50–400 feet deep, depending on the dynamics of the structure. That's 50–400 times more depth we need if we want a skyscraper kind of impact!

We better figure out, before we start building our new foundation, what we're going to be building on this foundation. For most of us, this is a brand-new exercise. How do we do it?

We need to find out three key things:
1. How deep does our foundation need to be?
2. What materials need to be used?
3. Where do we find these materials?

How Deep Do We Need to Go?

Let's think this through logically. We aren't going to know everything God has for us, but what we do know is we want to live out our purpose. By understanding that, we must also realize our purpose will be *big*. Not always big in others' eyes, but big to the greater plan God is working out on this Earth. Anything

> Anything that's in line with God's will is big and, if stewarded well, will continue to lead to even bigger things.

that's in line with God's will is big and, if stewarded well, will continue to lead to even bigger things.

Keep it simple. You know you're building something big (even though you may not know what yet), so what you know is your foundation has to be deep.

A second consideration may be to build a deeper foundation than we think we may need now to be able to support the future we may be trusted to carry out. If I build something more steady than is needed immediately, I can have space for God to pour more of His goodness out on top of it, and my foundation will still be able to handle it. More depth is always better than less. You never know when the depth will be used to hold up something more.

Question #1: answered.

What Materials Do We Need?

Well, all I know thus far in my journey of rebuilding is which materials can't hold up my future. I guess that's a start. So, how do I find out what to use to build the new foundation? The best way I know is to ask God first. I know this seems cliché, but we often run to the phone when we should be running to the throne. Ask God what to use. What people do you need to get around? What do you need to be reading? What groups can you connect with?

The reality is that we may never have intentionally laid a new foundation before. It is going to be awkward. We don't know what to do or where to go. Also, and this shouldn't be news, most people around us have never done this work either. Going to them for guidance is like asking a friend who has never been a parent how to raise your child. It doesn't work. Now, if you know a person who has done this work and can shed some light and wisdom as we gather our new materials for our new foundation, lean on them for sure. There is nothing like getting wisdom from those who have been down a similar path as we are beginning to go down, but if that person isn't in your circle today, that's okay, too. God is a pretty good resource, no matter what.

> Even when things seem trivial, they can be something God uses to build us up in the future.

Let's ask God to show us the people, places, and things He wants to use for our foundation to be solid. Even when things seem trivial, they can be something God uses to build us up in the future. I mean, who would've thought that little remark that my wife made when we bought our first house about it being "The Harper" floor plan would be a building block of a book to be published years later? I'll get to that story in chapter 11.

I will throw in a caveat here. If we think we have heard from God on something and it turns out we misheard or something didn't go as planned, that's okay. It happens. Sometimes, we miss some stuff. Go back to Him for clarity and continued guidance. We probably won't get it perfect the first time, but if we keep going back to Him for advice on what we need to be, He will honor that humility with wisdom. Remember, we don't just have God trying to guide us. The enemy loves to try and weasel his way into our thoughts to create opposition to the best plan for us, and at times, it can be confusing to know which thought or direction is right. Continually seeking God's wisdom can ensure that, even if we take the wrong path, we can correct it quickly.

The only thing I can guarantee as a key foundational material is that Jesus will need to be the Chief Cornerstone. Outside that, let His promptings and leadings guide you to find the right things to pour into your foundation.

Where Do We Find These Materials?

In Haggai 1:8, God tells the people, through Haggai, "Now go up into the hills, bring down timber, and rebuild my house..." Go up into the hills. The materials we will need to pour our new foundation won't be where we are today. We're going to have to go somewhere else, and it's going to need to be up. And if we notice, going up takes effort.

John Maxwell says it this way, "Everything in life worth doing is always uphill."

Nobody ever has lain down and rolled uphill. It doesn't work that way. We have to put in effort to get uphill. So, we can bet that the things we will need to build our new foundation will be in places where it will take effort to get them.

> "Everything in life worth doing is always uphill."
> John Maxwell

For me, one of those places was therapy. I began going to therapy in the fall of 2023. My wife had suggested it based on the stresses of my job for a while, but being a guy, I thought I could handle it. I know none of you are like this, but unfortunately, I was. When I began going to a Christian counselor, it was awkward. What were we supposed to talk about? How honest would I be? Would I be judged?

I'll get more into how counseling has helped me later in the book, but for this part, it's important to note where I had to find this piece of my foundation. I had to ask people at my church. Then, I had to go to a therapy office. Then, I had to meet with someone I never met. Then, I had to decide to be authentically transparent.

I had to do this while coordinating my work schedule to fit it in and pushing off other things I would've rather done. It was all uphill. But everything worthwhile in life is uphill, and I can say that that effort to go up was worth it.

So we have now found the materials we need and have an idea of how deep to go... How do we pour this thing to create the stability we need? The short answer often is slowly and with help.

Slow and Steady

We have all seen cement trucks, and if we pay attention to the pace at which the mixer is spinning on the back, it isn't super quick. If you've ever seen the concrete come out of the truck to the surface, it is coming out slow and steady. Not too quickly. Why? Because if it comes out too quickly, it tends to end up in the wrong spot, the contractors can't make adjustments as they go, and if something isn't right, it's tougher to correct once it's poured.

That's the same as when we begin to put down the new foundation of our lives, marriages, finances, or whatever we are rebuilding. It isn't going to happen overnight, nor should it. Consistency is greater than intensity in every case. Allow yourself the understanding that a little more of the right foundation poured in every single day will equal more stability over time. We should avoid the trap the enemy gives us by showing us false examples of people quickly seeing success in an area. When we are tempted to be discouraged by these, let us remind ourselves that what we are trying to build is not fast; it's forever. We tried it the world's way, and that's what got us here in the first place.

> Consistency is greater than intensity in every case.

The other side is "steady." Sometimes, because we don't see immediate results from a slowly poured foundation, it's easy to take steps backward or pause in the intentional rebuilding of our foundation. Every day, let's take steps, whether one or ten, to pour into our new foundation. That steadiness will allow for our foundation to be built solid to support where we desire to grow.

Let People Steady You

When we don't have it all together, we should be brave enough to say so. We talked earlier about asking God to put people around us who have gone through something similar, but this part is about honesty. Just because we told someone about this thing we're trying to do and they support us, that shouldn't be the end. We are going to need people who can steady us when we stumble. And we will stumble.

Asking God and godly people to stabilize us during this growth is not a sign of weakness; it's a sign of humble strength. We know that we don't know what the heck we're doing, and we'd rather look silly in front of people we respect and accomplish God's purpose for us than keep our weaknesses in the dark and settle for less than God's best.

That is godly humility, and that kind of wisdom is the stuff God can work through.

I remember that, as a kid, asking my coaches for help when I played baseball was easy. They were the coaches. I knew that was what they were there for. As I grew up, went to different-sized fields, faced new pitches, and swung larger bats, I needed help. And I knew it.

As adults, we somehow think that once we're out of the house, asking for help is not needed. We are programmed, either intentionally or unintentionally, that we should know what to do. And even when we do go to get guidance, it's often not from the right source. Picking our coaches well and then permitting them to coach us through this new foundation will help us have peace, knowing we have a source of wisdom in our corner who comes from a place of experience and good intentions for us. That's what coaches do. We just have to be willing to find them and allow them to do their job: coach.

The New Foundation Is Built Daily

John Maxwell once wrote, "You'll never change your life until you change something you do daily. The secret of your success can be found in your daily routine."

You see, our new foundations, while we are taking these initial steps, are just beginning. You and I will never be able to pour enough of a strong foundation all at once. Unlike a building or structure, as people, we get to add to our foundation every day. We get to decide to put God first in our lives every day. We get to choose to think a certain way about things every day. We get to decide to build our foundation with people who have good values and principles they live by every day.

> The secret of our success is found in our daily routine.

The secret of our success is found in our daily routine, and that will either move us inches forward or inches backward, but it will always move us.

Let's allow ourselves some grace when we miss the mark on a day, knowing we get another chance tomorrow. And let us be humbled when we go pour in some good foundational pieces some days, knowing our opportunity exists to build on that again tomorrow.

Our new foundation will be built each day, little by little, just like it was before. Only this time, we will build it with Jesus as the Chief Cornerstone, godly people as the support, and God's ways deepening our habits and thoughts to support the heights of a future we could've never imagined. Get ready; it's about to get fun!

CHAPTER 8

The Blessing Begins

Don't Despise the Days of Small Beginnings

When we moved to Houston, the church that we began to go to regularly was holding its services in a modified warehouse space. It was a smaller church, with about 250 people in regular attendance, and as we started to attend regularly, the growth was continuing at a rapid pace. We just happened to witness a season where it began to outgrow the space, and they had a campaign for a new building. This is not abnormal for a growing church, and they just recently got to a point where (a few weeks before I'm writing this) they held a groundbreaking ceremony on the land where our church will thrive. The anticipation for the groundbreaking ceremony had been building up for weeks. We looked forward to gathering with our family, praying over the land, and envisioning what God would do for our church community in that space.

As we drove out together on that Sunday evening, excitement was building. However, in the middle of the enthusiasm, a thought crossed my mind: *What exactly are we celebrating?* Here we were, driving out in the cold winter night, past our kids' bedtime, to an empty plot of land. It wasn't like we were celebrating the opening of the building. We weren't celebrating the first service in the new church. We weren't even celebrating getting the full funds to buy the land.

So what was it? What had brought about 150 people out, us included, to celebrate?

What we were celebrating was the groundbreaking!

What I found interesting was that the pictures we were taking were literally of shovels being put into the ground and moving the dirt. What we were celebrating as a church community was the beginning of the rebuild. We were not celebrating the end of the story; we were celebrating the beginning. We were focused on the future of what God was going to do through our faith move to lay a new foundation in a new place, to support new levels of growth in our church and its impact.

Interestingly, so many times in life, we want to wait until the finished product is complete to celebrate, but that's not how God operates.

Zechariah 4:10 tells us, "Do not despise these small beginnings, for the Lord rejoices to see the work begin…"

In our foundational story of Haggai, the Lord tells the people of Jerusalem,

> Think carefully about the day when the foundation of the Lord's Temple was laid. Think carefully! I am giving you a promise now while the seed is still in the barn. You have not yet harvested your grain and your grapevines, fig trees, pomegranate, and olive trees have not yet produced their crops. But from this day onward I will bless you.
>
> Haggai 2:18–19

It was not the day that the temple was complete that God promised the blessing. It was the day that the new foundation was laid.

So yes, we celebrate when things are complete. Finishing is most certainly better than starting. But the blessing and the celebration start when we begin. We've done the work to get rid of the old structure. We've done the work to leave the old place. We've done the work to rip up the bad parts of the old foundation. Now we're laying a new foundation, and we need to understand that the celebrations should start when that foundation is laid, not when the structure is complete, because our structure is never complete as we build our new temple.

So, why does this distinction matter? If the blessing starts with our new foundation, and since it may not feel like it, how can we install places of encouragement to keep us going in the right direction? Let's take a look at some practical ways we can ensure we are staying encouraged throughout our journey of building up.

Intentional Regular Reminders

When I was beginning my work on myself by going to regular therapy, I was experiencing a bit of tension. The tension was that I felt like therapy was helping, but then I had to live out life again with the same people and environments as I had for a while. As I began to realize my mindset was shifting, and I was building my foundation with the new tools I had been given to navigate life with, I asked my therapist how to use these tools more in daily life rather than retreat to what felt "normal."

What he told me changed how I navigated and allowed me to give myself grace.

He told me I had to do the weird, uncomfortable thing of reminding myself, almost minute by minute at first, that I am a new person with new thoughts, set up for a new purpose, given to me by God. For me, I often even did it out loud. I had to remind myself that God was blessing my new foundation and that intentional, regular confession gave me the strength to continue with what God was doing in me.

Here are some other examples of what this might look like for you:

1. Affirmations and declarations: Create personalized affirmations or declarations that remind you of your identity as a new creation in Christ. Repeat these affirmations regularly, either silently or aloud, to reinforce positive thoughts and beliefs about yourself.
2. Scripture memorization: Memorize Bible verses that speak to your identity and purpose in Christ. Recite these verses throughout the day to internalize God's truth and strengthen your faith. They don't have to be long, and there doesn't have to be a lot, but one or two that provide consistent reminders of who you are through Jesus will help more than you realize. Psalm 119:11 (NIV) reminds us, "I have hidden your word in my heart that I might not sin against you." Memorize Scripture to keep God's truth at the forefront of your mind.
3. Journaling and reflection: Keep a journal where you document your thoughts, prayers, and reflections on your journey of transformation. Write down moments of gratitude, breakthroughs, and prayers for strength and guidance. Being able to go back and read times when

you may have felt the grace of God or the peace He brought you can be so helpful in times when you are struggling to stay on your newly rebuilt path.

4. Accountability partnerships: Partner with a trusted friend, mentor, or accountability partner who can support you in your spiritual growth journey. Share your struggles, victories, and prayer requests with them, and hold each other accountable to living out your new identity in Christ. Proverbs 27:17 (NIV) shows us that "As iron sharpens iron, so one person sharpens another." Accountability partners help you grow and stay true to your spiritual commitments.

> *As iron sharpens iron, so one person sharpens another.*
> Proverbs 27:17

5. Prayer and meditation: Set aside dedicated time each day for prayer and meditation, focusing on God's presence and His promises for your life. Use this time to confess any doubts or fears to God and seek His guidance and strength. Remember that prayer is simply talking to God, and meditation is listening to Him. The honor we show Him by simply carving

out time to talk and listening to Him will help us navigate the world around us each day.

6. Visual reminders: Create visual reminders of your new identity in Christ, such as post-it notes with affirming messages or artwork that reflects your spiritual journey. Place these reminders in prominent places where you'll see them frequently throughout the day. We see enough stuff that tries to de-rail us from our intended direction, so we might as well put some intentional visuals in place to help correct the course if necessary.

These are just a few of the examples of the intentional ways we can ensure we are encouraging ourselves through this phase. While most of these are self-reflective, the right community can carry you through stages that may be tougher than others.

Community that Supports the New You

Lance Armstrong once said, "Community is strength." How succinct yet powerfully true that is. The community we surround ourselves with decides

> "Community is strength."
> Lance Armstrong

a lot about our direction. So, if we are laying our new foundation, we better ensure we are around people who are supportive of that move.

Full disclosure: as you rebuild, these will often be new people.

How do I know this? First Peter 4:4 tells us, "Of course your former friends are surprised when you no longer plunge into the flood of wild and destructive things they do. So they slander you." Oh, how true that will be, especially if the former friends Peter is mentioning aren't also rebuilding. Any time I am growing and the people around me aren't in that same process, there will be a number of them who will decide to peel away, gossip about me, and decide they don't want to grow. That's okay. It doesn't make them bad people, but it does give me a choice to make: Will I allow their lack of support to pull me back into old habits or attitudes that I am trying to rebuild for the sake of their approval, or will I continue to rebuild the temple of God that I am, to achieve the destiny God has for me and trust that He will bring new people into my life that will support the journey? This question will be tough, but when we know it's coming, we may be able to decide ahead of time what path to take. It doesn't mean I don't love the people I may be leaving behind; it just means my destiny is more important than their approval.

Embarking on the journey of rebuilding our foundation is no small feat, and it's essential to understand what it entails when it comes to those around us and how we can navigate it effectively. Here are some key points to consider:

1. Surround yourself with supportive people: Seek out individuals who will uplift and encourage you on your journey of rebuilding, especially now, when the full rebuild hasn't quite happened yet for all to see. While not everyone may understand or support your decision to reconstruct an area of your life, surrounding yourself with positive influences can make a significant difference. Look for friends, family members, or support groups who will walk alongside you and offer encouragement along the way.
2. Set boundaries: At this phase, it's crucial to set boundaries with individuals who may unintentionally hinder your progress. This may involve limiting time spent with people who bring negativity or temptation into your life. Communicate your boundaries respectfully but firmly, prioritizing your well-being and the rebuilding process.
3. Practice vulnerability: Vulnerability plays a crucial role in rebuilding your foundation. Be will-

ing to open up to trusted individuals about your struggles, fears, and aspirations. Sharing your journey authentically can foster deeper connections and provide valuable support and guidance. People know when we're trying to make our situation look easier or better than it is, and they withdraw their support because they feel like it's not needed. The only way we get the full measure of the support we need in this season is to open up to the right people when things get tough. I think we would be surprised to learn how many of the right people would be willing to lock arms with us.

4. Expect challenges: Human nature is to push back on things that may challenge us, so the same will be true when it comes to the people we will be around during our time of transformation. Odds are, a lot of them will push back on you in different ways. Be prepared to face challenges, setbacks, and moments of doubt. Remember that setbacks are a natural part of the process and an opportunity for growth and resilience.

> Committing to the process is more important than perfection.

5. Stay committed to growth: Rebuilding takes time and effort, but the rewards are worth it. Committing to the process is more important than perfection. Baby steps. Putting one foot in front of the other will help in continuing to grow. With growth, consistency is better than intensity. You may feel like you aren't making great strides every single day, and that's okay. What is important is to keep the person you're becoming in mind and commit each day to growing into that person, however small it may seem at the time. Keep your focus on the vision of the strong, resilient foundation you're building and the positive impact it will have on your life.

6. Lean on faith: Ultimately, lean on your faith in God as you navigate the rebuilding process. Trust that He is with you every step of the way, providing strength, guidance, and comfort. Draw strength from your relationship with Him, knowing that He has a plan and purpose for your life.

By surrounding yourself with supportive people, setting boundaries, practicing vulnerability, expecting challenges, staying committed to growth, and leaning on your faith, you can navigate the journey and more consistently be reminded that, while the work is never finished, the blessing has begun, and that's good news!

The Prodigal Son

Another story that comes to mind that is well known by many church-goers: The Prodigal Son.

The cliff notes version of the story is that a wealthy man's son decided he wanted his portion of his father's inheritance before his father's passing, so his father gave it to him. He proceeded to leave home and blow all his money on parties, women, and other frivolous things to have fun, but he ended up with nothing. He was in such bad shape that he ended up feeding pigs for a local farmer and was so hungry that the slop the pigs were eating looked appetizing to him. Then, the Bible says, "He came to his senses."

He just came out of a life of paying prostitutes, wild living, and blowing all of his family inheritance. He got so low that he just decided to go back home to his father. He didn't even consider himself worthy to go back as his father's son, but was willing to go back, even as a servant. He wasn't perfect as a person yet, but his changing his heart posture to humility was laying a new foundation.

The son just turned back home. He just took the first step. He began to lay the foundation.

As he was laying his new foundation, his father responded by running towards him even though he was still far away.

This story has so much nuance to it, but I find it very interesting that the Bible specifically says that as the son was walking back to his father's house, his father saw him from a far distance and, filled with joy and love, ran to him.

The Father didn't care about the distance; what allowed him to be filled with joy was that his son changed his direction.

I believe that is what God cares about, too. I believe He isn't as concerned with how far away you are from perfection but more about what direction you are moving in. Are we running away from God with our decisions or running to Him? The job's not done, and that's okay. It's not about perfection. It's about progress.

> The Father didn't care about the *distance*; what allowed him to be filled with joy was the son changed his *direction*.

Perhaps Paul said it best in his letter to the Philippians when he wrote,

> I don't mean to say that I have already achieved these things or that I have already reached perfection. But I press on to possess that perfection for which Christ Jesus first possessed me. No, dear

brothers and sisters, I have not achieved it, but I focus on this one thing: Forgetting the past and looking forward to what lies ahead, I press on to reach the end of the race and receive the heavenly prize for which God, through Christ Jesus, is calling us.

Philippians 3:12–14

He hadn't finished his structure yet, but pressing forward was his focus. He learned that reaching his desired state of perfection was less important than continuing to focus on the direction he was moving.

Promotion Doesn't Require Perfection

Let's look at a more worldly example—a job promotion. Anytime somebody gets promoted at a job, they've usually been working very hard. They've been trying to climb to the next step of their career path, and they find themselves up for a promotion, so they apply for it and ultimately end up getting it.

It's interesting that when the promotion happens, the day that I find out I get a promotion, I am celebrated. I celebrate with myself. I celebrate with my wife. I celebrate with my friends. I celebrate with my coworkers, my future coworkers, and my team.

Yet no boss waits until they decide that an employee is good at the job to begin paying more money. Nobody waits until I've been in the job for five years to say, "Okay, you're complete. You're a complete version of this type of employee; therefore, we're going to start blessing you now." That's not what they do. A new foundation is laid in your career. A new foundational expectation is laid; therefore, the blessing begins that day.

This is a real-life example that I've lived through: When I got my job as VP of Sales, I had previously been a Sales Executive based in Jacksonville, Florida. When I got that VP job, my compensation went up, as most promotions are tied to, but my first year in that job I didn't know what the heck I was doing. Like, I really didn't know. I had no idea what I was doing, and yet they still blessed me with more money every two weeks. I wasn't a complete VP. I wasn't a perfect VP. I hadn't built the structure yet. Some days, I didn't even know if I could spell VP. I did not know how to be the perfect version of this new thing, and yet, the blessing started with the promotion on the first day that my new foundation was laid.

So, I want to encourage you. The blessing will begin as you are laying your new foundation. You don't have to have the structure complete yet. You need to make sure that your foundation is laid properly so that it can align with the blessing that you're wanting and what God has in store for you.

For me, my foundation lies in Jesus (as if you couldn't tell by now), but it wasn't always that way. In the past, that foundation was built with other things, like money or titles. Other times, it was built with relationships. In really dark times, sad to say, it was built with alcohol, status, or accomplishments.

In my experience, I can tell you that foundations built on sand will quickly demand either repair or rebuild. For the longest time, I found myself opting for repairs—it was the easier route, after all. But here's the thing: repairs are temporary. They might patch things up for a while, but sooner or later, the cracks start to show again.

If I keep choosing to repair instead of rebuild, I'm stuck in a cycle of constant maintenance. But when I choose to rebuild, I do it once and for all. I lay down a new foundation, solid and sturdy. And as my journey unfolds, I continue to pour strength into my life, reinforcing that foundation day by day.

With a strong foundation beneath me, my purpose and impact can flourish, reaching new heights with each step forward. So, let's commit to building something lasting, something resilient—a foundation that can weather any storm and support our purpose for years to come.

The Foundation Is the Multiplier

Jesus tells a story in Matthew 13 that illustrates how important the foundation is in the story of a farmer scattering seeds. Matthew 13:3–8 says,

A farmer went out to plant some seeds. As he scattered them across his field, some seeds fell on a footpath, and the birds came and ate them. Other seeds fell on shallow soil with underlying rock. The plants sprang up quickly, but they soon wilted beneath the hot sun and died because the roots had no nourishment in the shallow soil. Other seeds fell among thorns that shot up and choked out the tender blades. But some seeds fell on fertile soil and produced a crop that was thirty, sixty, and even a hundred times as much as had been planted.

The seed was the same. The soil, or foundation, was the difference-maker in the harvest.

Similarly, in life, our foundation acts as the soil for our growth and success. A weak foundation may yield some results, but they will be limited and fragile. On the other hand, a strong foundation provides the stability and nourishment needed for our endeavors to flourish. Just as rich soil supports healthy plant growth, a solid foundation multiplies our ability to achieve our goals and aspirations, producing abundant fruits of our labor.

> The seed was the same. The soil, or foundation, was the difference maker in the harvest.

So, what is the multiplier in the situation you're trying to rebuild?

Maybe it's for your marriage. Maybe your marriage is built on a foundation right now of just seeing each other when we see each other, two ships passing by each other with all the other obligations and responsibilities that come with work and kids. We are just going with the flow. We got a lot of stuff going on. We've got kids, so we have soccer and football; we have to make it to dance and fit in band, and we're running so fast that we're just trying to keep up. We're trying to get by day to day, and our foundation is like, "Just get by day to day so we can make it until tomorrow." I have found myself in those seasons where the foundation seems to consist solely of surviving the daily rat race of parenthood with young children.

If your foundation is built on worldly pursuits or distractions, such as money or status, then the communication in your marriage will likely only yield a limited harvest. However, if your foundation with your spouse is rooted in intentional connection and genuine attentiveness, it can bear fruit of a different magnitude.

Imagine a marriage where intentional conversation and active listening are the building blocks of your relationship. When your spouse speaks, you not only hear their words but also respond with genuine care and action. You prioritize meaningful interactions over distractions, such as putting down your phone and looking your spouse in the eyes, fully present and attentive to their needs.

This kind of marriage is aligned with God's plan for relationships—a partnership built on love, respect, and mutual support. By investing in this type of foundation, you create a fertile ground for growth and intimacy in your marriage, allowing God's blessings to flow abundantly in your relationship.

Apply this principle to everything. You can apply it to marriage. You can apply it in friendships. You can apply it in employment. You can apply it when running a business. You can apply it in your faith. You could apply it to anything you want. Wherever we build a more stable foundation, intentionally align our actions with our beliefs, and strive to live the life God has planned for us, we will get a higher multiplier.

Better Foundation = Better Result

Let's consider a couple, John and Emily, whose marriage journey reflects the transformative power of rebuilding their foundation.

At one point in their relationship, their marriage was characterized by a shaky foundation of deceit, unresolved conflicts, and self-centeredness. John was deeply engrossed in his career, often neglecting household chores. When Emily would clean the house, John's initial reaction was one of impatience and entitlement. Often, he would think, *It's about time. I've been asking for the house to be cleaned for weeks.* He failed to recognize her efforts and instead harbored resentment, viewing her actions as an obligation rather than a gesture of love.

However, as they committed to rebuilding their marriage on principles of honesty, forgiveness, and mutual respect, their dynamic began to shift. Now, when Emily cleans the house, John's internal dialogue is filled with appreciation and admiration. He recognizes the significance of her efforts and expresses genuine gratitude for her contribution to their family life. When he thanks her, it comes from a place of sincere appreciation, and Emily feels truly valued and cherished.

John saw Emily perform the same action: cleaning the house, but now, with a stronger foundation, the result was John showing genuine gratitude and Emily knowing it was heartfelt. This shift in response now led to a greater blessing for their marital structure to continue to grow strong.

Same action. Different result.

The same becomes true of our journey when we rebuild an area of our lives that puts God first. We have done the work, and God is now at the center. The blessing has begun, and the reward in our daily lives is promised. Now we get to build up our new structure, and the materials we choose will be important.

Work Left to Do

Wouldn't it be awesome if God's blessings would just rain down from heaven? Sometimes, that's what I find myself expecting, but that is rarely how He works. When the foundation is laid, it doesn't necessarily mean you're going to see the blessing right away.

I will go back to the book of Haggai, where the scripture says the Lord promised a blessing while the seed was still in the barn. Interesting timing. Why promise the blessing so far in advance of when the people would see it? I believe it was meant to show us that when we prioritize laying the foundation for His temple first, the same seed that had only given limited harvest before will now have God's blessing on it, and so will the harvest.

However, it still meant that the farmer had to sow the seed into the field. He still had to do the work. It just meant that God was going to bless the process more now because the foundation of the temple was laid.

For whatever reason, God has chosen to partner with us in this journey called life. He often requires us to do what we can do while He takes care of what we can't. In this illustration in Haggai, only God can bless the harvest, but the people are still responsible for sowing the seed.

As we begin to see the foundation be rebuilt and realize that the blessing of God may begin to be in our lives (although we may not yet see the manifestation of it), let us not forget that we still have a part to play. We are responsible for creating the structure of the temple so it is sturdy upon the new foundation. If we don't know what part is ours and what part is His, the simplest thing to do is to ask Him. James 1:5 tells us, "If you need wisdom [if you want to know what God wants you to do], ask our generous God, and he will give it to you. He will not rebuke you for asking."

> If you don't know what part is yours and what part is His, the simplest thing to do is to ask Him.

Asking God what to do in this partnership of rebuilding will provide us with clarity as we build up the structure of our lives in a renewed way to better prioritize Him and allow us to walk in the purpose for which we were created. Time to build up!

CHAPTER 9

Your New Structure

Materials Matter

"They don't build them like they used to," was my grandfather's favorite line.

When I was a boy, our family vacations always included visiting family. With not a lot of time or resources, the time and money we did have was spent driving up to Indiana to visit my mom's side of our family for a week each summer. My sister and I made the drive as fun as we could, playing the license plate game or "I spy" until we got tired of it and began to try and sleep the rest of the way. On a twenty-hour road trip from Florida, you run out of things to do pretty quickly. Luckily, the landscape provided on the drive up I-75 from Florida to Indiana allowed us to soak in some sights. The mountains of the Appalachians were something to behold for a kid who grew up in Florida and then came the farmland of Kentucky and Indiana. It was amazing how so much land could spread so far, with perfect rows of corn or beans as far as the eye could see.

When we finally got to my grandparents' house, I remember thinking, even as a young kid, how amazing life was there. The stars at night looked so close you could reach out and touch them. When it was quiet, all you heard were the sounds of nature whispering peace into your soul, whether through crickets chirping or the sounds of corn stalks rubbing up against one another in the breeze. Catching fireflies was a highlight of each trip, as we only saw them when we came to visit the family. It seemed like this was such a simple yet amazing way to live.

Inevitably, we would go "into town" for a day, and my cousins and I would be able to pick out a toy to buy from a local store and bring it back to the farm to play with for the week. Being the 5–14-year-old boy I was (depending on the year), it was only a matter of time before I would be a little too rough, and the toy would break. I'd bring it to my dad or grandfather to try and fix, and without fail, my grandpa would say, "They don't make them like they used to."

While I didn't understand at the time, I now know he grew up with toys made of metal. Tinker toys in his day were made of solid wood or metal, so breaking them wouldn't be an easy task.

I think that old-school thought process may be beneficial to us as we begin to choose what will form part of our new structure. How will we think? Who will we associate with? What habits will we create? As we answer these questions, we can apply some practical things to assess what the new materials can be that will give us the best chance to build the structure the way we want it to last.

> We may need to go *up*.

In our foundational book of Haggai, God tells His people in chapter 1, verse 8, "Now up into the hills, bring down timber, and rebuild my house." Like with our foundation, I believe the materials He wants us to rebuild our structure with may not be at our current level…we may need to go up. So what does going up look like practically? Here are just a few places we can start.

1. Community or support groups: Joining a community or support group focused on personal development, mental health, or overcoming specific challenges can provide invaluable encouragement and accountability. These groups offer a safe space to share experiences, gain insights from others, and receive support during difficult times.

2. Therapy or counseling: Seeking professional therapy or counseling can be instrumental in facilitating personal growth and healing. A qualified therapist or counselor can offer personalized guidance, tools, and techniques to address underlying issues, develop healthier thought patterns, and navigate life's challenges more effectively. This can be strange at first (it was for me), as therapy sometimes has a stigma that comes along with it among certain people. But once we realize this is simply a place to go to get the new tools we don't have or get access to new ways of thinking that can help us healthily build our structure, it becomes much more beneficial than we realize.

3. Educational workshops or seminars: Attend workshops, seminars, or webinars on topics related to personal development, emotional intelligence, and mindfulness. These educational opportunities provide practical strategies, insights, and exercises to cultivate self-awareness, resilience, and positive habits. If we think about it, we were in classes our whole lives until we were out of school to learn how to do the things we didn't yet know how to do. Then, when we become adults, somehow we think that we should just know how to be married, be a parent, deal

with stress, or do any other of the thousands of adult things that come along with life. So usually, we just look to those around us, or our parents, to show us the way. This comes with challenges, so allowing ourselves to get outside our comfort zone and proactively get educated in the areas that can help us build our pillars will help us get a fresh perspective to be able to evolve.

4. Books and podcasts: Explore books, podcasts, and audiobooks that offer inspiration, guidance, and practical advice for personal growth and self-improvement. Even the right YouTube videos can be helpful. Choose titles authored by experts in the area that resonates with where you're rebuilding. The ability to get access to education online is unlike anything in history, and yet most of us use it for things that distract or entertain us. While a good TikTok scroll may be helpful to disconnect every once in a while, we should recognize that everything we take in imparts pieces of our new structure, and, if we're willing to, using these sources as a place to build and support our new structure can be very beneficial.

5. Find a Bible-based church: Find and engage with a local church that aligns with your beliefs and values. A community that is accepting and

that has gone through (and is continuing to go through) its own journey of rebuilding will be able to offer spiritual guidance, support, and a sense of belonging as you navigate your journey of rebuilding. It can also offer hope and grace when we may fall off track or make a wrong turn along the way while encouraging us to stay the course of putting our structure up intentionally.

6. Fitness or wellness centers: Incorporate regular exercise and wellness activities into your routine by joining a gym, yoga studio, or fitness class. Physical activity not only promotes physical health but also contributes to mental well-being, stress reduction, and overall resilience. We are going to need all of these things as we continue to build our structure.

7. Volunteer opportunities: Get involved in volunteer work or community service initiatives that align with your values and interests. Contributing to the well-being of others can foster a sense of purpose, fulfillment, and connection while providing valuable opportunities for personal growth and self-discovery. You'd be surprised at how much giving helps you.

Pillars of Our Structure

While our structures are built daily, minute by minute, and by many different things, there are some intentional pillars we can create on our new foundation that can help us stay solid as God's temple. We will never get everything right. Nobody does. But if we do our best to ensure the pillars are solid and intentionally built correctly, we will be able to make adjustments when mistakes happen more easily. There are four main pillars to get our structure solid.

Pillar 1: Our Association

Proverbs 13:20 shows us, "Walk with the wise and become wise; associate with fools and get in trouble." Seems simple, but it's not always easy. Put differently, Jim Rohn once noted, "You're the average of the five people you spend the most time with." Our association is a pillar of what we're building, and an extremely important one, but how do we find this association that can be wise in the areas we're trying to rebuild?

The simple answer is that they may not be in your circles now. Remember, we are instructed to "go up into the hills." That may mean doing the work of getting out of our comfort zone to find the people we want to walk with. It may mean seeking people out through

> *Walk with the wise and become wise; associate with fools and get in trouble.*
> Proverbs 13:20

church or work that you may not have had a relationship with prior. If you're in a place where it isn't as easy as meeting someone new, maybe, for a season, your association is authors of books you read or podcasters you listen to that pour life into you in an area. Whatever you need to do to get an association that's aligned with who you are now becoming, it will be worth the work to find them and associate with them as much as you can.

Pillar 2: Our Thoughts

Paul makes it simple in Philippians 4:8, helping us know what we should focus on when he says, "And now, dear brothers and sisters, one final thing. Fix your thoughts on what is true, and honorable, and right, and pure, and lovely, and admirable. Think about things that are excellent and worthy of praise."

While this sounds great, how does that translate practically? If I am rebuilding my health, maybe I need to fix my thoughts on the excellent state of taking care of my body to be able to enjoy a long life with my family and friends. Maybe it's focusing on what I can add to my diet that's giving me energy and making me feel healthier rather than indulging in too many sweets or snacks. If I am rebuilding a relationship, maybe I can concentrate on starting my conversations with that person with positive assumptions rather than looking for something wrong to prove someone isn't trustworthy.

A simple hack could be to think about what you're thinking about. Is it constructive to your end goal of rebuilding in an area, or is it off track a bit and could need some adjustment? This pillar is going to take some practice, as are the next two, because we have thousands of thoughts per day, and a lot of them can be on autopilot from previous experiences. Daily practice with auditing how we think about a situation can help us build this pillar to handle the big future we're headed toward. This intentionality behind our thoughts will ultimately drive how we talk to ourselves.

> Think about what you're thinking about.

Pillar 3: Our Words

In another gem from King Solomon, he writes in Proverbs 18:21, "The tongue can bring death or life; those who love to talk will reap the consequences."

Life and death seem to be pretty heavy consequences of our words at first glance, but modern science is proving that this biblical wisdom is correct.

In their jointly written book, *Words Can Change Your Brain*, Dr. Andrew Newberg, a neuroscientist at Thomas Jefferson University, and Mark Robert Waldman, a communications expert, state, "A single word has the power to influence the expression of genes that regulate physical and emotional stress." My words dictate whether I'm stressed or not.

Furthermore, according to these two experts, exercising positive thoughts can quite literally change one's reality. So when I combine my words with my thoughts, the reality of the world I experience changes. I began to see a world full of good people, not that everyone wants to take advantage of me. I begin to look for the good things in life, and whatever we look for, we find.

It's like whenever I want to buy a new car, I tell my wife what I want. I research what it looks like, so I think about it more. I potentially tell other family and friends about what I think I want to get. So, inevitably, I begin to see this car on the road...all the time. I mean, where did all these come from? It seems like everyone I am driving alongside has this car in different colors, with different options, from different years.

What happened? Did the car company suddenly have a flood of sales in the prior weeks? Did people who owned that car all of a sudden move within five miles of where I would be at all times? Of course not. It was my thoughts and words creating the reality that I saw. The same number of those cars were on the road before; I just wasn't looking for them.

Our words matter to our rebuilding more than we often realize, so our willingness to be intentional with them, even if we sometimes don't feel like we agree at the moment, can create the stability of this third pillar in our new structure.

Pillar 4: Our Habits

Australian-born author F. M. Alexander once famously wrote, "People don't decide their futures; they decide their habits, and their habits decide their future." How true that often is. When I think of myself when I begin a rebuilding journey, I often wonder, *How did I get here?* Maybe you have had that thought, too. It wasn't like I set out for this; it just kind of...happened.

Could it have happened because we developed habits, without intentionality toward a result, that led to where we are when we discover it's time to rebuild some things?

> *"People don't decide their futures; they decide their habits, and their habits decide their future."*
> F.M. Alexander

In his award-winning book *Atomic Habits*, James Clear shares how powerful our habits are. In an interview in 2019, he expanded on his book's findings when he shared, "Habits are among the most important topics to understand in life. This is true of every person in every situation. Your life is filled with habits. Research shows that 40 to 50 percent of your actions on any given day are automatically habitual. But the true influence is even greater because your habits often influence the conscious actions that follow. You pull your phone out of your pocket out of habit and then spend the next ten minutes consciously responding to email or scrolling social media. The habit influenced both the initial action and the ten minutes that followed."

When we take inventory of those automatic things we do each day and then audit whether or not they're helping us rebuild ourselves or whether they may be serving the old version of ourselves, we may quickly see pockets where we can make adjustments and begin to create new habits that can continue to serve us and our new selves and our new structure. This pillar is a game changer.

Once we have our pillars beginning to take shape, we will be surprised at how many things fall into place. It doesn't mean we will get everything right, but with the foundation built properly and now the structural pillars being built with intention, we will begin to see ourselves, God's temple, being built in such a way that the details are more easily falling into place.

Detail Consistency

God seems to care very much about the details of our lives based on what we see in scripture. The details used by Solomon in 1 Kings, describing the details of the temple he built for God, are down to the minute detail. In Exodus, we see the detail God used when instructing Moses to build the Tabernacle of the Covenant to get down to the precise measurements and the exact place the materials were to be taken from. Why would this kind of detail need to be seemingly micro-managed by God?

> You have done the hard part; now let's make this baby shine!

I think it may be because, once we have God first, Jesus as our foundation, and pillars solidly in place, to do a half-baked job on the details would be a terrible waste of work potential. You have done the hard part; now let's make this baby shine!

A Rhythm of Asking

Joshua is one of the most interesting stories in the Bible to me. This man was one of the twelve spies originally chosen by Moses to scope out the Promised Land. He was one of the two who insisted that they go in and take the land as God instructed, despite the challenges that may await them, and had to pay the price of the disobedience of the rest of his people by spending forty years in the wilderness due to other people's distrust in God's direction. Once that generation dies off and Moses passes away, God charges Joshua to lead the people across the Jordan to the Promised Land. He obeys every detail that God asks of him as he leads the Israelites across the Jordan and marches around Jericho seven times. The wall falls at the sound of their shout on the seventh day, and the city falls, all due to Joshua's amazing boldness and obedience in following God's direction at each step, as crazy as it may have seemed at times. (I'm sure his men were questioning his sanity for the seven days they marched around the walls in silence.)

Defeating Jericho was a massive accomplishment in the mission toward the conquest of Canaan, one that had been in the works for over forty years, and it was done because of Joshua's faith and his willingness to ask God what to do at every step and do it to the best of his ability. But something interesting happened right after that.

> Don't forget to ask God for direction in the details.

There was this little city just to the east that he wanted to conquer as well called Ai. When he sent spies to the city, they came back and told him it was a small town and that it should only take a few thousand soldiers to capture it. Nothing they couldn't handle, especially given the magnitude of their most recent victory. But when they went into Ai, Joshua 8:24 says, "...they were soundly defeated." Later in the chapter, it tells us the Israelites were stricken with fear due to their defeat by such a seemingly small city. How could they lose? They had just taken Jericho, a city fortified by its mighty walls, and now they were "soundly defeated" by the men of this small town. What happened?

Joshua made the mistake that I often make and that many of us will make during this time of rebuilding: He forgot to ask God for direction in the details. See, when he prayed after this defeat, God would reveal that a man in his army by the name of Achan had sinned against the Lord by stealing some of the things God asked them to set apart for Him. That little detail caused God's favor to be lifted from Joshua and the Israelites until it was rectified. That small thing needed to be dealt with before God could continue to bless them on their quest toward Canaan.

Thank God we live in a time of grace, where we can be forgiven by Jesus' sacrifice for us, so we don't have to "correct" things as they did before Jesus' gift to us, but we should learn from this story. God wants to be involved in every aspect of our lives, and He would like to be consulted for each of these aspects, too. There is nothing too small that God doesn't want to be involved in. If we aren't going to Him for what we consider details, we will often come up with our own plan that is inconsistent with what, when, how, or where God wants us to act in a certain situation, and that's when we get a less than desirable result.

I often find myself going to God for the big stuff. Should I take this new job? Should I move cities? Should I spend my money this way? How can I help a family member who is hurting? How can I parent my kids better? These kinds of big things are often a no-brainer to ask God for guidance on, but I wonder how many times I could have avoided a mess I created by simply asking for direction in the details of everyday life that could've prevented harm in the other end of it.

See, the foundation and the pillars are big to us because we operate in the human capacity, but they're small to a God who is all-knowing, all-powerful, owns and controls everything, and has our life in His hands. See, in the context of God being able to deal with it, it's all small. It only takes a breath of His favor to change a circumstance that seems big to us. It only takes a touch of His hand to create generational blessings. It only takes a work of His wisdom to change a heart.

> It only takes a breath of His favor to change a circumstance that seems big to us.

If we want to avoid some unintended pitfalls as we're rebuilding our new structure, we would be wise to remember that whether things seem big or small to us, God can handle it all with the same amount of sovereign ease, so going to Him for everything is a rhythm that is worth creating, even for direction in the details.

The New You

CHAPTER 10

The Withholdings

Blessings Aren't Lost, Simply Withheld

As we continue to witness the fruits of our rebuilding efforts and embrace the peace that accompanies knowing we're constructing something lasting, there's a natural inclination to seek the full benefits of this transformation. The good news? The rewards far exceed our expectations.

Have you ever encountered someone who recently underwent a profound transformation, seemingly attracting blessings and success at an exponential rate? It's as if they've tapped into a hidden reservoir of favor and abundance. We often wonder: What did they do differently? Is this level of favor attainable for me, too?

The answer is a resounding yes. If we've reached this stage in our rebuilding journey, we're well on our way to experiencing extraordinary blessings.

Reflecting on the words of the prophet Haggai sheds light on an important principle. In Haggai 1:9–10, God chastises His people for neglecting the reconstruction of His temple while focusing on their own success. He says,

> You hoped for rich harvests, but they were poor. And when you brought your harvest home, I blew it away. Why? Because my house lies in ruins, says the Lord of Heaven's Armies, while all of you are busy building your own fine houses. It's because of you that the heavens withhold the dew and the earth produces no crops.

Notice the distinction: God withheld His blessing, not out of punishment but as a consequence of misplaced priorities. If it was gone forever, He would have said something like "took" or "stopped the crops from thriving." Instead, he withheld them. When we prioritize self-centered endeavors over honoring God's purpose, we inadvertently create barriers to receiving His abundant provision.

God's promise of exponential blessings is contingent upon aligning our efforts with His divine plan. As we rebuild our lives on a foundation of faith, service, and truth, we position ourselves to receive blessings that transcend mere material gain. Instead of fleeting rewards, we unlock lasting favor and spiritual abundance.

Let's embrace this profound truth: The path to exponential blessings begins with a heart dedicated to God's purpose in all areas of our lives. By investing the time and intention of rebuilding ourselves in places, we invite divine favor and abundance into our lives, transforming every aspect with enduring grace. That is what rebuilding is all about, and the payoff is well worth the journey!

Withholding vs. Losing

In a season 1 episode of the '90s sitcom *Friends*, Rachel is shown getting a paycheck from her first job while living in New York City. Her excitement of beginning her journey of not living off her father's dollar shows through as she opens the paper envelope to see what she earned in that pay period. Excited to share the moment in front of her friends in their favorite coffee shop, her excitement quickly dwindles as she realizes the realities of adulthood. Her comment in the moment of disappointment is relatable to all who learn what tax withholdings look like.

She grimaces as she asks, "Who is FICA and why are they getting all my money?"

In the context of tax refunds, withholding serves as a mechanism to ensure financial responsibility and compliance with tax obligations. Throughout the year, a portion of our income is withheld by the government to cover anticipated tax liabilities. At the end of the year, when we submit our tax returns, they're evaluated by the governing body, the IRS. Depending on how we have stewarded our income, it is determined whether we paid too much, too little, or just enough in taxes based on the withholdings throughout the year. This process, although often viewed as an inconvenience, often culminates in a tax refund—a return of the withheld funds once the tax evaluation is complete and the governing body of the IRS has determined we are due that refund.

Similarly, when we examine the principle of withholding in a spiritual context, we can draw parallels to how God interacts with us. Just as taxes are withheld to fulfill obligations, God may withhold blessings or favor when our priorities are misaligned.

God's withholding is not punitive but strategic. It signifies a pause in the release of His blessings until we demonstrate alignment with His divine plan. When we prioritize worldly pursuits over spiritual growth or potentially neglect our relationship with God, we inadvertently create barriers to receiving His abundant provision. He does this not to punish us but because if He were to release what He has for us when

> God's withholding is not punitive but strategic.

we aren't putting Him first, it could destroy us in ways that would be tough to recover from.

The analogy of tax refunds underscores an essential truth: Withholding does not equate to loss; it signifies a temporary delay until the appropriate conditions are met. In the same way, God's withholding is an invitation to realign our lives with His purpose and priorities.

When we place God first in our lives, honoring Him with our resources, time, and devotion, we position ourselves to receive His blessings abundantly and without delay. Just as tax refunds are released once taxes are settled, God's blessings flow freely when we prioritize His kingdom and seek His will above all else.

The Difference in God's Economy

The best news of all is that we serve a God who operates in far more abundance than this world can imagine (and thank God He is far more graceful and kind than the IRS). When we delve into the Scriptures, we encounter profound examples of God's restorative power and generosity. In the story of Job, for instance, we witness God's extraordinary provision as He not only restores Job's fortunes but doubles them, showcasing divine abundance in the face of adversity.

Similarly, in Isaiah's prophecy to the people of Israel, God promises a double portion for their former trouble—a testament to His capacity to multiply blessings beyond measure. This divine multiplication transcends human comprehension and underscores God's limitless ability to redeem and restore.

Ephesians 3:20 encapsulates the essence of God's abundance beautifully, emphasizing that His capabilities exceed our wildest dreams or expectations. This verse invites us to envision a reality where God's blessings flow in exponential measure, far surpassing anything we could conceive or request. It reads, "Now all glory to God, who is able, through his mighty power at work within us, to accomplish infinitely more than we might ask or think."

In God's economy, the concept of withholding is not a signal of scarcity but an opportunity for unprecedented multiplication. When God chooses to release blessings that were previously withheld, He does so with unmatched opulence and magnificence. His intention is not merely to restore but to transform, elevating our circumstances to levels of abundance that defy human limitations.

As we reflect on these biblical truths, we are reminded of God's un-

> In God's economy, the concept of withholding is not a signal of scarcity but an opportunity for unprecedented multiplication.

wavering faithfulness and His desire to bless His children abundantly. The examples in Scripture serve as compelling evidence of God's extraordinary generosity and His commitment to bestowing blessings that exceed our expectations, especially now that you have put Him first and rebuilt His temple in such a way that honors Him.

Let us embrace the promise of Ephesians 3:20 and approach God with hearts filled with expectation, knowing that His plans for us are marked by abundance and His provision is boundless. In His economy, the return of withheld blessings is not just a restoration but an invitation to experience His infinite grace and magnificence.

The Withholding is a Blessing—Even While Withheld

The withholding that God enacted in our lives served as a profound act of divine grace and wisdom. When God withholds blessings, He does so not out of neglect or indifference but out of a deep desire to ensure that our priorities align with His will. In His infinite wisdom, God knows that receiving His blessings prematurely, before we have rebuilt our lives according to His design, may hinder our spiritual growth and development. Like women who give birth: If the blessing of the baby comes prematurely, the odds of survival go down the more premature it is. The same is true in seasons when other blessings are withheld while we are still busy clearing out the old structure and rebuilding ourselves.

Here are some ways God uses the season of rebuilding to our benefit:

1. Divine guidance and intention: God's withholding of blessings reflects His divine guidance and intention for our lives. He knows us intimately and understands what is truly beneficial for our spiritual well-being. When God withholds certain blessings, He is guiding us toward a deeper understanding of His purposes and a realignment of our priorities with His kingdom.
2. Promoting spiritual reflection: The period of withholding serves as a time of spiritual reflection and introspection. It prompts us to examine our hearts, motives, and desires in the light of God's truth. This introspective journey allows us to identify areas where our priorities may be misaligned and provides an opportunity for repentance and growth.
3. Building dependence and trust: God's withholding fosters a deeper sense of dependence and trust in Him. When we experience delays in receiving certain blessings, we are invited to trust in God's timing and sovereignty. This process

strengthens our faith and reliance on His provision rather than on our efforts or desires.
4. Cultivating humility and surrender: Embracing the season of withholding requires humility and surrender to God's will. It humbles us to acknowledge that our plans and desires must align with His purposes. Surrendering to God's timing and agenda allows Him to work more deeply within us, transforming our hearts and minds according to His divine will.
5. Preparing for greater blessings: God's withholding is not a denial of blessings but a preparation for greater blessings ahead. As we rebuild ourselves as temples of the Holy Spirit, prioritizing His kingdom and righteousness, we become vessels ready to receive His abundant grace and favor. The process of rebuilding involves spiritual growth, character development, and alignment with God's purposes.

God's withholding is a testament to His love and commitment to our well-being. By withholding certain blessings, He prompts us to examine our hearts and priorities, fostering a deeper sense of reliance on Him and His kingdom. This period of withholding is not a punishment but an opportunity for introspection and spiritual renewal.

During this rebuilding, God invites us to reevaluate our motives and desires, discerning whether they align with His divine purpose. He desires to cultivate in us a heart that seeks Him above all else, recognizing His kingdom as the ultimate source of fulfillment and blessing.

As we embrace this season of withholding with humility and surrender, we position ourselves to receive God's blessings in their fullness. The process of rebuilding ourselves as God's temple involves relinquishing our self-centered desires and embracing His divine plan for our lives.

> God desires to cultivate in us a heart that seeks Him above all else.

Ultimately, God's withholding is a manifestation of His grace and mercy, guiding us toward a deeper relationship with Him. As we commit to putting God first and rebuilding our lives according to His design, we prepare ourselves to receive His blessings in abundance, leading to a life of purpose, fulfillment, and divine favor.

How to Re-Gain the Withholdings

When my daughter was five, she got her first tablet to help entertain her while taking long trips to see her grandparents. (I know…some of you are judging already, but stick with me; there is a point to this story beyond whether or not that was a good decision.)

As she became older, she got time where she could watch it periodically at home. Whether it was for finishing all her chores, being nice to the kids in the neighborhood, or something that was over the top, she would get rewarded with being able to watch it. As tablet time began to slowly increase, however, what my wife and I found was that she became more distant from us when she was on it. She would zone out, and this screen would be the only thing she cared about.

We decided we needed to help her shift her priorities, so we began to withhold some things from her if she wasn't putting her family first. We knew she wasn't intentionally doing this, but as a five-year-old, she wasn't able to discern the importance of her relationship with us and her brother over what felt fun at the time.

While she threw a bit of a fit early on (at times, this would be an understatement), she began to get back to her old self, and the excitement of hanging with the family overrode the frustration of not having the thing she wanted. She began to ask for it less and less until, finally, when she would ask periodically and we said, "No," it didn't seem to faze her much. She still remembered it was there, but whether she got to enjoy it or not didn't matter as much because her priorities had shifted. Since then, not only has she been able to enjoy it more, but she knows that when we regulate it, it is not for punishment, but it is our discerning love knowing that too much of a good thing is not a good thing, at least for the ultimate family connection we are trying to create within her and the rest of our family.

> Too much of a good thing is not a good thing.

That's how God's withholding works in our lives, too. When we are living to please ourselves and our agenda, often even without realizing it, God is loving enough not to let us enjoy the fullness of what He has for us unless we are putting Him first. Like with our daughter, it's not punishment; it's protection. It's protection from our human desires overtaking the relationship God wants us to enjoy with Him because when we put Him first, all the other things that are added to our lives become that much sweeter. Jesus taught us this in

> *Seek the Kingdom of God above all else, and live righteously, and he will give you everything you need.*
> Matthew 6:33

Matthew 6:33, when He said, "Seek the Kingdom of God above all else, and live righteously, and he will give you everything you need."

To keep God first as you rebuild your life's structure, here are some practical steps you can take to guard yourself from slipping back into previous patterns:

1. Evaluate your priorities: Just like we observed our daughter's behavior, take a moment to evaluate your priorities. Are there things in your life that are taking precedence over your relationship with God? Identify any areas where your focus may have shifted away from God. This is an ongoing process and something we all can be doing consistently to ensure we are doing the best we can to prioritize properly.
2. Set boundaries: Similar to how we established boundaries with our daughter's tablet use, set intentional boundaries in your life. Ask God what those boundaries should be. He knows your heart, your strong points, and areas where you may be more susceptible to fall. Work with Him to determine specific times or situations where you will prioritize spending time with God. This could involve setting aside dedicated time each day for prayer, reading the Bible, or worship.
3. Practice self-discipline: Encourage self-discipline in your daily routines. Challenge yourself

to put God first in more and more things until He is sought in all decisions and actions. This might mean choosing to attend a church service or small group gathering instead of other activities that conflict with your spiritual growth.

4. Create accountability: Just as we provided guidance and accountability for our daughter, seek accountability in your spiritual journey. Connect with a mentor, friend, or spiritual advisor who can support and encourage you in putting God first. This usually has to be done intentionally. It may seem awkward at first, but it pays huge dividends if we have a person or people in our corner to keep us encouraged and accountable toward the best direction for us.

5. Shift your focus: Over time, redirect your focus from worldly desires to spiritual growth. Like our daughter rediscovering the joy of family time, find ways to rediscover the joy of fellowship with God. Yes, this will take time. The Bible tells us that as you prioritize Him, you'll begin to experience the fullness of His blessings and presence in your life.

By implementing these practical steps, you can actively keep God first as you rebuild your life's structure. If you notice, though, a lot of these ways to create guardrails in your prioritization are self-reflective, so honesty will be crucial. Remember, it's not about punishment but about protection and deepening your relationship with God, which ultimately enriches every aspect of your life. Going through these steps to help yourself keep priorities in line while making excuses, justifying, or ignoring an area or two isn't going to do you any good. After all, this journey is about you and for you. Be honest with yourself…it's the only way these steps work in your favor.

Consistency Compounds

As we build our new structures and take intentional measures to ensure we are aligning with God as our priority, we will find there is a bit of a bell-curve effect that happens. The first day or week, it may not feel like much of a difference. Especially once we have our foundation solid and pillars in place, the day-to-day of building our new structures can feel a bit mundane. Like nothing is happening. It's been said that success is boring, and that's how this may feel. But what we may find is that we are simply stacking consistent days, one after another, on our newly formed journey, and that consistency becomes something God can trust with the supernatural.

In his book *Atomic Habits*, James Clear titles it "The Power of Tiny Gains." In his graph below, he shows how impactful stacking small wins on top of each other can be, and the same is true of stacking the daily decisions on top of one another to create a life of stability and a temple of God that can receive what God has for it, because of the way we're building it. He uses basic quantities for the illustration, and we can see that, as the days pass, initially, it may not look like much, but it is the consistency that creates the compounding effect. This shows the impact of just getting 1 percent better every day for a year versus getting 1 percent worse each day for that same year. It may not feel like it, but the tiny daily gains add up.

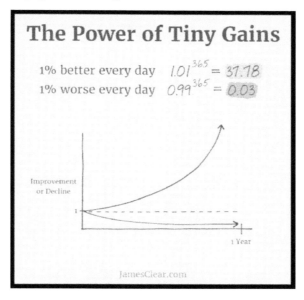

God has things held back for us. He did this to protect us, not to punish us. He did this to ensure that, when we got the destiny He created for us, we would have the foundation, the pillars, and the structure to be able to steward it well and not lose it. After all, since we are rebuilding ourselves, God's temple, then it would make sense for Him to ensure we don't build it just to have it in ruins again down the road. And finally, He did it so that when we prioritize Him by building our lives with Him first, the next generation may look at us as an example of building His temple with an eternal lens and have a blueprint of how to continue to do the same in their lives.

CHAPTER 11

Passing It On

Show and Tell Is Better Than Just Tell

Ever noticed that whoever follows you duplicates more of what you do than what you tell them to do? Whether it is your children, your employees, or just friends who look up to you, people tend to do more of what they see than what they're told.

It may be because people trust the truth, and our actions tell them who we are. Actions tell them who we are, and words tell them who we want to be. When our words and our actions align, we have created something trustworthy, and it becomes even that much more attractive. It's called integrity, and it's often a rare quality in worldly

> Actions tell people who we are, and words tell them who we want to be.

matters today. When we commit to doing our best to exhibit it, the value it passes to people who follow us is immense.

According to a study published in the *Journal of Personality and Social Psychology*, children are highly observant of their parent's behavior, and they tend to imitate what they see. This phenomenon is known as observational learning or modeling, a concept introduced by psychologist Albert Bandura. Children learn social behaviors, attitudes, and values by observing and imitating significant role models in their lives, particularly parents.

In workplaces, employees are more likely to adopt the behaviors and work ethic of their leaders than simply follow directives. This is known as the "leadership shadow" effect, where employees mirror the actions and values of their supervisors or managers.

Moreover, research conducted by the Harvard Business School found that leaders who demonstrate integrity, transparency, and fairness in their actions build stronger trust and credibility among their teams. Employees are more likely to emulate these positive behaviors and contribute to a healthier organizational culture.

Real-world examples further illustrate this principle. Consider the impact of influential figures like Mahatma Gandhi or Martin Luther King Jr. Their actions spoke volumes about their beliefs and values, inspiring countless individuals to follow their lead in advocating for social justice and nonviolent resistance.

Therefore, when it comes to influencing others, whether it's children, colleagues, or friends, our actions serve as powerful catalysts for change and growth. By living out our values and principles authentically, we create a lasting impact and set a compelling example for those around us to emulate. And now that we have intentionally rebuilt, the confidence of knowing it'll be an emulation we want to pass on is a sweet bonus!

The "Why" Lasts, the "What" May Vary

When I began to become interested in cooking, I was about sixteen or seventeen years old. I began to take to it, mainly because I learned it was a good way to impress girls, if I'm honest. As I continued to experiment in the kitchen, I found that I was learning what to do but was lacking the reasoning behind it. As I knew "what" to do, I knew recipes, could watch a *Food Network Show*, and do a pretty good job of duplicating the chef, but as soon as the exact instructions left, so did my ability to execute the dish. I didn't know why the ingredients were what they were, why the amounts were so much, or why they cooked in certain ways for certain times. All of it was more confusing once I was left to my own devices, and it all came to a head when I tried to bake my girlfriend brownies in my twenties.

As a pretty broke twenty-something, recently out of college, I wanted to impress my girlfriend, who was visiting from out of town, by baking her brownies for after this homemade meal I had copied from a fancy food show I watched the week before. I printed out the ingredients and directions that week and bought the ingredients at the store for both the meal and the dessert. Saturday came for me to impress, and I was ready.

The meal turned out fantastic! I made a filet mignon with a cognac cream sauce (that flambé got me bonus points), truffle mashed potatoes, and roasted Brussels sprouts drizzled with balsamic reduction. I probably spent all the money I had for this to turn out well, so good thing it worked. Bonus: My girlfriend was distracted enough while I was cooking that she didn't notice I used my printed directions. So I thought I had fooled her into thinking this was all me.

Now that the meal went over well, it was time to make dessert. Super fancy: boxed brownies. Three ingredients in the directions seemed simple enough, but I had only two of them. I didn't have an egg. Um...what do I do? I can't drop the ball now. So, I did what any self-respecting person trying to figure something out would do...I googled it.

"What can replace an egg when baking brownies?"

The answer I found said to substitute one tablespoon of vegetable oil.

I add the oil to the mixture, put it in the baking dish, put it in the oven at 350 degrees, and set the timer for forty minutes as instructed. When I checked it after that time, it was still not cooked. I left it in for another five minutes and checked again. Still not solid in the middle. I gave it ten minutes and checked again. Same result. This went on for an additional hour after the original forty minutes; all this time, both my girlfriend and I wondered what was wrong.

After about two hours, we decided to take it out and realized the bottom and sides of these brownies had burnt to a crisp sticking to the sides of the dish, but the center hadn't set. The dessert was ruined.

Was it the oven? Were the instructions wrong? Why wasn't it cooking?

It was the oil. When I didn't have the exact ingredients to get what I wanted and didn't have the knowledge of why ingredients go in or don't go in something, I messed up the whole thing.

Here is the lesson for lasting change: People need to know the principles more than the prescription.

When we pass down to the next generation how to build themselves to be able to support the destiny God has for them, we must tell them more about why we're doing what we're doing than telling them exactly what to do. The main reason is obvious but rarely considered. We aren't going to be here for every part of their life. We will have a lot more time away from people to whom we will pass on these principles than we have with them. When they aren't around us to know the exact ingredient to add to build their foundations well, or how to choose the pillars they're building around, their ability to seek God's guidance and discern what to do based on knowing the reason why you did what you did during your rebuilding, is going to help them in making the decisions to do one thing over another.

> People need to know the principles more than the prescription.

Passing on the Foundation

In chapter 5, we talked a lot about how much early experiences shaped our foundation, and it will be no different for those who are now following you. Their experiences will be a key component of what their foundation will be.

I don't know about you, but the thought of someone following me can, in some areas, be a little intimidating, especially in areas we are rebuilding and haven't always gotten right. Just know that we won't always get it right, and we are going to need to lean on God's grace through the process, up to and including passing on some of the things we want to instill into others. There are some basic steps we can take to better guide us as we begin to pass along some of the reasons and some of the "why" we built the foundation we have newly created.

1. Model integrity: Show honesty and integrity in your own actions and decisions. For example, admit when you make mistakes and demonstrate how to take responsibility and learn from them. Saying sorry first goes a long way, especially in a society that isn't always quick to admit fault. This simple action can be a game changer in what you leave in the next generation. You can take this to the next level by explaining why it is important to apologize and admit mistakes in relationships as you're trying to build trust and respect.
2. Encourage kindness: Engage in acts of kindness together, such as volunteering at local charities or helping neighbors in need. Explain the impact of these actions on others, and allow questions to be asked openly around it. Helping our next generation have a more well-rounded perspective that others in the world are hurting allows for them to go through life with a less entitled

and more compassionate heart. Explaining that we are kind because Jesus taught us to do this, regardless of how others act, so we can show love to others as Jesus shows it to us allows for the why of kindness to be understood deeper.

3. Model values and beliefs: Have open discussions about values, beliefs, and life lessons during family meals or dedicated times for conversation. Encourage children to express their thoughts and ask questions and catch them behaving in line with these values and beliefs to further encourage that being duplicated. Catching people doing the right thing is one of the most powerful tools for influencing them to repeat this positive behavior. Additionally, modeling values and beliefs don't always mean those following us will follow blindly. Allowing for questions and healthy conversation around why these beliefs and values are what they are allows all involved to know you're not trying to control them but simply modeling the values you believe will help build them up for the purpose their future holds.

4. Set boundaries: Establish clear boundaries and guidelines for behavior and explain the reasons behind them. Consistency in enforcing boundaries and explaining their role in the formation of their foundation helps children understand

expectations. The previous story of my daughter and her tablet is a great example of what that could look like in a parental setting. This also exists in some of the best corporate environments in the world. Companies know that if their new employees, who are following senior leadership, get outside the created boundaries to ensure consistency with company values, they either need to be coached to get back on track or, potentially, the employee will need to find a new place to work. These boundaries may seem stringent, but it's all to protect the foundation of yourself that you have worked so hard to rebuild. Believe it or not, people respect boundaries set with loving reasons more than we realize.

5. Provide guidance: Offer support and guidance when children face challenges or conflicts. Help them develop problem-solving skills and resilience. In addition, when you're trying to solve an age-appropriate challenge, bring your child into the conversation to let them watch you deal with challenges. It will also encourage them that even Mom and Dad have tough things they face, too, and watching them see part of the resolution process when emotions aren't too high, allows them to see you reasoning out a solution in real time. Word of caution here: This should

only be something that you are trying to solve that is not a marital issue or anything that could jeopardize the family dynamic. This should be things like showing them how you talk through how to best talk to a neighbor who is difficult or how to deal with a situation at work that doesn't align with the values you've created. How do you work through these types of things? Watching how you think will allow them to begin to foster a thought pattern of their own, with your influence as a guide.

6. Read and discuss stories: Use books, movies, or real-life stories to illustrate important principles like perseverance, compassion, and courage. Discuss the lessons learned from these stories together. Even personal stories of how God has come through in your life and throughout your journey will serve as a foundational addition to the lives of those coming after us when they hit times when they need hope and direction.

Having some practical ways to ensure our foundation is being shown and pockets to explain the reasoning behind it will absolutely make the difference in the next generation being able to navigate the building and potentially rebuilding their foundations if needed, as they grow into the person God called them to be.

Passing on the Pillars

When my wife and I bought our first house, the house was still under construction. We were so excited, as all young couples are, to have been moving into our first house in St. Augustine, Florida, and we knew this house was meant for us (or at least my wife did). You see, the floor plan of the house that we bought was called "The Harper" floor plan. "If that isn't divine, I don't know what is," in her words. It was at the end of a *cul-de-sac*, and it was a beautiful four-bedroom, three-bath farmhouse-style home on a large lot overlooking a lake…gorgeous! We were also buying right at the beginning of the COVID-19 pandemic, so, needless to say, the builders wanted it off their inventory just as much as we wanted to take it off their inventory.

Because the house was still under construction when we bought it in April of 2020, and it was not going to be ready to move in until June of that year, we had to sit in our small apartment, day after day…and wait. When I say that I have never driven by a construction site as much as we did during that time, I'm not exaggerating! We drove by probably four to five times a week to check up on the progress. While we were anxious to move in, it was such a fun time for us, and it was so exciting to watch the house go up. We watched the inside get walls, doors put in, and windows put around the home.

The exterior of the porch was enclosed, and a fence was put around the yard. We could just envision our kids (one of which we had at the time and another was on the way) making memories in this place. We couldn't wait to move in!

What I noticed, though, as the house was being built, was that the construction site was very messy. There were tools everywhere. Cans of paint and extra drywall shavings throughout the house. Dust for miles. Even the driveway and the yard had things lying in it as it was being built.

> Construction sites are very messy.

What hit me was that the structure that I had to trust to protect and shield my growing family was built by people who would not live in it. You see, when something's built by people who are not going to live in it, their goals and objectives during the build are completely different than if they were going to live in it after their build is done.

The same is true for us as we pass along our new structure to those coming after us. We will often have times when the busyness of life impedes our ability to build our structure perfectly or that may not always align with our pillars the way we want. We will have times when our words, our association, our thoughts, and our habits aren't showcasing what we want passed on, because, after all, we are human. In those times, it's important to have some tools in our bag to ensure that the next generation catches the good things as much as possible and understands when we go astray to stay on the right path for them and their future.

Here are a couple of things we can do to increase the likelihood we pass on the structure that can build a strong future for those coming behind us.

Consistent Communication

Regularly communicate your values, beliefs, and aspirations to your children, employees, or mentees. Use everyday conversations, stories, and experiences to reinforce positive behaviors and attitudes. Even if you stumble or make mistakes, openly discuss them and share lessons learned. A great way to do this is to incorporate daily discussions at the dinner table or around the end of the day with your family. We use these three basic questions with our kids each night that begin to open up the conversation:

1. What went well today?
2. What was tricky or tough to navigate today?
3. What do you want me to know about today?

These three basic questions are asked of and answered by everyone at the table, adults and children alike, and allow for a forum to share, learn, and grow through everyday life.

For employees or mentees, have regularly scheduled times where they see your willingness to be vulnerable with your imperfection while also coming back to the structural elements of habits, association, thoughts, and words that took place and why they were aligned properly, or maybe what you would've done differently given the chance. This regular communication lets people know that just because we rebuilt how God asked us to, it doesn't mean we will always get it perfect, and when that happens, it isn't fatal.

Create Teachable Moments

Look for opportunities to teach valuable lessons through everyday activities. One effective strategy is to encourage individuals, especially children, to actively engage in self-reflection and perspective-taking during everyday activities. For example, when a child performs a kind gesture for a sibling, pausing to discuss the emotional impact of that action can enhance their understanding of empathy and pro-social behavior. Research in devel-

> Look for opportunities to teach valuable lessons through everyday activities.

opmental psychology highlights the importance of experiential learning and its impact on behavior.

Empathy and brain development: Studies have shown that practicing empathy can influence brain development, particularly in regions associated with social cognition and emotional processing. When individuals engage in perspective-taking exercises, such as imagining how their actions affect others, they activate neural pathways involved in empathy. Over time, repeated engagement in such activities can strengthen these neural circuits, leading to greater empathy and interpersonal skills.

Impact of experiential learning: Experiential learning, which involves learning through direct experience and reflection, has been shown to enhance learning retention and behavioral change. When individuals actively participate in discovering the consequences of their actions, they are more likely to internalize the lessons learned. This approach fosters a deeper understanding of cause-and-effect relationships and promotes critical thinking.

Behavioral modeling and mirror neurons: Another fascinating aspect of teachable moments is the role of mirror neurons in observational learning. Mirror neurons are brain cells that activate both when we act and when we observe someone else performing the same action. By witnessing positive behaviors and their outcomes firsthand, individuals can internalize these experiences and replicate similar behaviors in future contexts.

Long-term impact: By incorporating teachable moments into daily interactions, parents, educators, and mentors can facilitate long-term behavioral change. Research suggests that repeated exposure to reflective learning experiences can shape moral reasoning, decision-making skills, and emotional regulation in children and adolescents. These foundational skills contribute to healthy social and emotional development.

Creating teachable moments involves more than just telling individuals what to do—it involves guiding them through experiential learning and self-discovery. By leveraging scientific insights into brain development and behavior, we can optimize these opportunities to nurture empathy, perspective-taking, and positive behavior in the next generation. The combination of intentional guidance and immersive experiences can yield lasting effects on personal growth and character development.

Encourage Positive Associations

Foster environments that promote positive, God-focused associations. Surround yourself and your family with supportive, like-minded individuals who embody the values you cherish. Attend community events, workshops, or seminars that reinforce positive attitudes and behaviors to reinforce the desired strength of the pillars. Here are a few areas we may want to pay attention to.

Free Time Associations

In free time settings, such as recreational activities or family outings, prioritize environments that cultivate positive relationships and experiences. Encourage participation in sports teams, clubs, or hobby groups that align with the pillars and structure you'd like to see modeled in your child or mentee. These settings provide opportunities for children and adults alike to interact with peers who share similar goals and values, fostering a sense of belonging and camaraderie. Additionally, family-oriented activities like nature walks, game nights, or volunteering together can strengthen family bonds and promote positive associations with shared experiences.

Structured Time Associations (School or Church)

During structured activities like school or church, emphasize the importance of choosing environments that support positive character development. Engage with educational institutions and religious communities that prioritize values such as empathy, integrity, and compassion. Encourage participation in extracurricular programs, youth groups, or service projects that reinforce ethical principles and social responsibility. By actively engaging in these settings, we can build meaningful relationships with peers and mentors who exemplify positive behaviors and attitudes.

Online Associations

In today's digital age, online interactions play a significant role in shaping social connections and behavior. Encourage responsible and positive online associations by monitoring digital content and platforms accessed by family members. Encourage participation in online communities, forums, or social media groups that promote constructive dialogue, creativity, and mutual respect. Emphasize the importance of digital citizenship, including ethical use of technology, respectful communication, and critical thinking skills when navigating online spaces. By fostering positive online associations, individuals can leverage technology as a tool for learning, collaboration, and positive social interaction.

Fostering positive associations across various settings—free time activities, structured environments like school or church, and online interactions—creates a supportive foundation for personal growth and character development. By intentionally curating social environments and engaging in meaningful interactions, individuals can reinforce shared values, build supportive relationships, and contribute to a culture of positivity and godly structure that will be able to support the future they have in store.

Share Your Story

English novelist Rudyard Kipling once noted, "If history were taught in the form of stories, it would never be forgotten." And isn't that the goal? We want our story to be something the next generation can glean from and go back to and reference when they need it. It is no coincidence, then, that Jesus was the greatest storyteller of all time. He created imagery and illustrations in the minds of His followers that would stick with them long after they were gone, and here we are, over two millennia later, still quoting them as if just spoken. Also, it is interesting that, in His stories, He shared the whole thing, not just the parts that people wanted to hear. He wanted to help us, not entertain us. He was also very discerning about when to share what parts so as not to overwhelm His audience when He

> *"If history were taught in the form of stories, it would never be forgotten."*
> Rudyard Kipling

deemed them not ready. So when we share our story, doing so in a compelling and wise way will make all the difference.

Timing Is Everything

Jesus was big on timing. He showed us this in His conversation with His disciples in John 12:16 (NIV), when He says, "There is so much more I want to tell you, but you cannot bear it now." Jesus knew that timing was important. He had the discernment to realize where His disciples were and what they could handle and apply. The same should be our goal as we guide the next generation. Let's try and pay attention to where the receiving person is, and continually be prayerful to ask God to show you when to talk about certain things and when to hold back. This is especially true when having a teaching conversation. While our heart is in the right place, trying to get something to sink in while in certain mental, emotional, or relational states has the potential of falling on deaf ears or, worse, of being taken as criticism, leading to rebellion, all because we unintentionally timed the conversation or interaction poorly. Here are some guidelines to help determine the appropriate times for these important interactions.

> Jesus was big on *timing*.

When to Have Teaching Conversations

1. Calm and receptive states:
   - After a positive experience: Following a shared success or joyful moment, such as after a family outing, a sports victory, or a completed project, people are generally more open to reflection and learning. Use these times to reinforce the values demonstrated during the activity.
   - Quiet times: During peaceful moments, such as bedtime routines or quiet Sunday afternoons, individuals are more likely to be in a contemplative and receptive state. This is an ideal time for sharing stories and values.
2. Natural teachable moments:
   - Real-life scenarios: Utilize real-life situations as teaching opportunities. If your child shows kindness to a friend or perseveres through a challenge, discuss the importance of these actions immediately after the event. Over-rotation toward something positive will always stick with someone and make them want to experience that feeling of someone being proud of them again, which will often lead to that behavior being repeated.

- During reflection: Encourage discussions during times of reflection, such as family dinners or dedicated family meetings, where everyone is invited to share their thoughts and feelings openly.
3. Structured learning times:
    - Scheduled family discussions: Designate regular times for family discussions where values and lessons can be imparted in a structured manner. This could be a weekly family meeting where everyone knows that the agenda includes learning and sharing, or it could be something as informal as a dinner discussion at the end or beginning of a week. The important part is to have fun while also leaving with a sense of growth. If someone feels like they're reporting to a meeting for accountability's sake or to check the box, they will loathe it about as much as a lot of adults do in the corporate world. Make it valuable.
    - Educational activities: Integrate teaching into structured activities like reading together, watching educational programs, or engaging in community service, where lessons can naturally emerge from the activity itself.

When Not to Have Teaching Conversations:

1. High-stress or emotional situations:
   - During conflict: Avoid trying to impart lessons during or immediately after a conflict. High emotions can cloud judgment and openness, leading to resistance or misunderstanding. This may take longer than we desire at times, especially if the conflict is deeply rooted in something that doesn't have a simple resolution. If there is a lengthy resolution needed, waiting, even for a while, will still get us better results than trying to rush for the sake of urgency.
   - Stressful times: When individuals are under stress from school, work, or personal issues, they may not be in the right mindset to receive feedback or lessons. In these settings, focus on helping them get back to a place of peace and stability. It shows we care more about them than we do about what we're trying to impart to them. Always remember that people need to know they come first as an individual. People

> People don't care how much you know until they know how much you care.

don't care how much you know until they know how much you care.

2. Busy and distracted moments:
   - During hectic schedules: Attempting to teach or share stories when someone is busy or focused on a task can be distracting and ineffective. Wait until they have the time and mental space to engage fully. This can be tough nowadays, with so many of us having packed schedules in the name of busyness. It may require us to become part of their schedule. Maybe set up a time to have lunch or put time on the calendar to go to dinner. If they are chronic schedulers, this may be a good option to allow their schedule not to impede the ability for us to pass on key lessons that could make a lasting impact.
   - In the middle of activities: There is nothing worse than someone interrupting what you are doing to try and shift over to something they want you to focus on. It is one of the ultimate signs that we don't value them and think our agenda is more important than theirs. Avoid interrupting enjoyable activities, such as playing a game or watching a favorite show, to impart lessons. This can cre-

ate a negative association with the teaching moment.

3. Uninvited feedback:
   - Unsolicited advice: Be cautious about offering feedback or lessons when they haven't been asked for. Even well-intentioned advice can come across as criticism if it's not sought after. I have heard it said that unsolicited advice is most often taken as criticism. The same can be true of ill-timed conversations around the pillars we are striving to instill in the next generation. People have different personalities, so some people may be more open to this than others. But it's always better to air on the side of caution when it comes to giving feedback without it being requested.
   - Non-emergent situations: Unless it's a situation requiring immediate correction for safety or ethical reasons, it's often better to wait for a more opportune time to discuss the lesson. Often, we think the feedback we want to give is more important than it is, so being prayerful about how urgent this conversation is will be helpful.

Practical Examples

1. Positive experiences:
   - After a successful team project at school, discuss the importance of teamwork and perseverance over a celebratory ice cream outing.
   - During a relaxed evening after a family hike, share stories about the values of nature appreciation and physical wellness.
2. Natural teachable moments:
   - When your child helps a neighbor, praise their kindness and discuss how helping others is a core family value during a quiet dinner that evening.
   - Use a family game night to emphasize the importance of fair play and integrity when someone follows the rules or shows good sportsmanship.
3. Structured learning times:
   - Establish a Sunday evening ritual where each family member shares a lesson they learned that week, fostering an environment of continuous learning and reflection.
   - During a regular family meeting, discuss upcoming community service projects and how they align with the family's values of compassion and service.

By being mindful of timing and context, we can ensure that our teaching conversations are more likely to be well-received and effective, helping to build the pillars we want to pass on to the next generation.

In this chapter, we've explored the importance of timing our teaching moments, creating environments that foster positive associations, and leading by example. By being intentional about when and how we impart lessons, we can ensure that our teachings are more likely to be received with an open heart and mind. We've also highlighted the significance of maintaining supportive communities and engaging in meaningful activities that reinforce our values.

As we journey through the process of rebuilding our lives and creating a solid structure rooted in faith, it's essential to remember the legacy we leave behind. Passing on our values, habits, and principles to the next generation is a part of this journey that is very humbling and is an honor that is bestowed upon us to give to those who are following behind, whether children or adults. While we may not always model perfection, our efforts to teach, guide, and inspire those who follow us will have a lasting impact.

As you continue to rebuild your structure, remember that the foundation you lay today will support not only your future but also the future of those who look up to you. Embrace the responsibility of being a role model with grace and humility. Your actions and words have the power to shape lives, instill confidence, and inspire greatness.

Passing it on is not just about teaching; it's about living authentically and consistently. It's about showing up, even when it's challenging, and demonstrating the values you hold dear through your everyday actions.

When we seek God first and align our lives with His purpose, we create a ripple effect that extends far beyond our immediate reach.

In the end, the legacy we leave is not measured by material success but by the character, faith, and resilience we instill in others.

> In the end, the legacy we leave is not measured by material success but by the character, faith, and resilience we instill in others.

Let's commit to rebuilding ourselves into people who honor God, support our loved ones, and inspire future generations to live with purpose and integrity. The journey of rebuilding is ongoing, but with each step, we move closer to the abundant life that God has in store for us and those who come after us.

Conclusion

The journey of rebuilding is definitely a road less traveled. I think this is why, when we see people who have done the work, they are so attractive to us. Their willingness to dig in and rebuild in an area has created someone who has both empathy for the current situation we're in and the knowing and experience that we can rebuild to be the temple of God we desire to be.

I hope this book has provided you with the insight that God made you for a purpose. I hope He spoke to you individually as you read the words on these pages. I hope you know He is right there with you, rooting you on to the life He created for you. And I am rooting you on, too.

He has given us all the gift of free will, and when we are willing to use our free will to do His will, life begins to evolve into the best version it can be.

It has been my great honor to pour into you during this time together. I hope you walk away with the encouragement to rebuild where needed, the practical ways to get through each season of your rebuild, and are inspired to continue on the journey toward your purpose. Mostly, I hope you walk away knowing that you're so valuable to God that He asked a complete stranger to write this book for you. You're special. You're unique. You're worthy. Embrace it!

About the Author

Jon Harper is a coach and leader who has been a leader for over a decade throughout the United States. He has led within the walls of both corporate and private sector organizations and has developed some of the strongest teams within those organizations by rebuilding them over the years. Jon has a passion for helping others find their purpose and helping them with practical and applicable steps to realize their potential. Jon has been recognized as a Marquis Who's Who in America recipient for his consistent work in leadership throughout the years and is known for using biblical principles in leadership to turn teams and people in the direction of success to experience lasting change.

www.ingramcontent.com/pod-product-compliance
Lightning Source LLC
LaVergne TN
LVHW022339160125
801481LV00003B/5